T0380801

WHOLEHEARTED

Living a Life Devoted to God As Outlined
in Colossians 1

MARY LYNNE WEBB

WestBow
PRESS®
A DIVISION OF THOMAS NELSON
& ZONDERVAN

WestBow Press books may be ordered through booksellers or by contacting:

WestBow Press
A Division of Thomas Nelson & Zondervan
1663 Liberty Drive
Bloomington, IN 47403
www.westbowpress.com
844-714-3454

ISBN: 979-8-3850-3673-8 (sc)
ISBN: 979-8-3850-3672-1 (e)

Library of Congress Control Number: 2024922160

Print information available on the last page.

WestBow Press rev. date: 11/07/2024

CONTENTS

ACKNOWLEDGMENTS

First and foremost, I thank God for all He is and all He has done.

Thanks to Annie for being God's instrument to encourage me to attempt this task.

Thanks to Samantha, Sarah, Ali, Elizabeth and Judy for proofreading the text and making suggestions.

Thanks to Bryan for all the messages he has shared from God's Word.

Thanks to my daughter-in-law, Elizabeth, for encouraging me.

Thanks to my family and our extended family as well, for a lifetime of memories and thousands of stories, the good, the bad, and the ugly.

Thanks to **all** the people God has placed in my life who have taught me valuable lessons.

INTRODUCTION

For a long time, the word "wholehearted" has been a source of conviction to me. I stand amazed at the accounts of people who scripture characterizes as having a wholehearted devotion to God. Caleb, who along with Joshua, believed God's promise when the rest of Israel was afraid of the giants. David, a man after God's own heart, was clearly a fallible person. And interspersed among the evil kings of Judah were kings who served God wholeheartedly among stubborn, rebellious people. I have wanted to have that kind of relationship with my Savior. I have struggled, and continue to struggle, with my own stubborn and rebellious self. I have wondered why this is so difficult. As I write down what I believe God has led me to write, I am writing and studying for myself. If, by His grace, He allows me to share this with you, then I will trust that He has a purpose in that. I hope to be honest with you about my own struggles, so that you can learn from my mistakes. I ask that you be honest with yourself as well. I hope to share some small victories, so that you can see that all is not hopeless. I ask that you praise God in joyful celebration of the victories He has given you. And I hope to share some lessons I have learned as an observer of those around me.

(Last week, my co-worker, friend, and prayer partner, Annie passed me in the hallway of the school where we work. She said "I had a dream, and it was so real. You had written a book. I want to read it when you finish it." I tried to think of a plot for a Christian novel but could not come up with anything. But, as she was leaving yesterday afternoon, she clarified that her dream was about a book with spiritual insights. That brought "wholehearted" to my heart and mind again. Which brings me to one of my own struggles. I get up every morning early with the purpose of reading the Bible before I go to work. But I have a real temptation to check social media, weather apps, our bank balance, news, etc. instead of actually spending the entire time with God. This Saturday morning, I woke up 30 minutes before my workday alarm clock to a terrible headache and almost constant lightning. I came into the kitchen for caffeine to help the headache. I sat down, picked up my laptop, not my Bible. But there was NO internet. So, I picked up my Bible. I am in hopeful anticipation of what God reveals to me.

Please, I implore you, to search the scriptures for yourself. While I do believe that God is leading me to write this, and that He will teach me through this study, I do not believe that what I write is infallible. Study the scriptures that I have given for reference. I also urge you to read the surrounding verses to have a better understanding of what the scripture is addressing in each passage. Unless otherwise noted, all scriptures are from the New International Version of the Bible.

- Acts 17:11 New International Version (NIV) 11 Now the Berean Jews were of more noble character than those in Thessalonica, for they received the message with great eagerness and examined the Scriptures every day to see if what Paul said was true.

This has long been one of my favorite verses, and one by which I try to live. I urge you to be of noble character, examining the scriptures daily to see if the words I write are true.

CHAPTER 1

WHOLEHEARTED COMMITMENT

I would say that most of us probably know in our hearts that our commitment to God should be wholehearted, but I'm not sure that we have taken the time to explore exactly what having a wholehearted commitment means, why it is important, the consequences of not following God completely, or the blessings of being true disciples.

As a sort of pretest, write a definition of what you think being wholeheartedly devoted to God means?

According to the New Oxford American Dictionary (New Oxford Dictionary)

> **Wholehearted** (adjective)–showing or characterized by complete sincerity and commitment

To put this in the context of our walk with Jesus, we *could* say, "We have a complete and sincere commitment to Jesus." But that only scratches the surface. When the Holy Spirit dwells in us, being wholeheartedly committed to Him means that our entire lives–every word, every thought, and every action are not only committed to Him, but that He Himself works through us as we yield ourselves to Him.

Read Galatians 2:20

Is a life wholeheartedly committed to God something we achieve or something we allow God to do? It is a purposeful surrender, a volitional yielding, and a choice to humbly submit. We cannot be wholehearted in our relationship with Christ only by our actions. God does not force us to serve Him as unthinking robots. We must choose to allow Him to work through us. I am writing this on Memorial Day weekend. My son is active duty in the military. He has lost two friends who we remember this weekend. Our military men and women willingly yield their lives for our country. There is no draft. They are not compelled to serve. It is a choice they make. Then they become part of a greater entity. They obey the rules and commands. They become disciplined for their safety and the efficiency in their missions. They work together, each having their own purpose yet willing to give up their own lives for their buddies. In a similar way we choose to submit to God, then we can be used by Him for His purposes. We want to obey Him. We are part of His body, the church. We consider others above ourselves.

According to the New Oxford American Dictionary (New Oxford Dictionary)

submit (verb)–accept or yield to a superior force or to the authority or will of another person

In order to begin to live a wholehearted relationship with Jesus, we must first accept Christ as Savior, yield to His authority, and recognize His superiority.

HIS SUPERIORITY AND AUTHORITY

Examine the following scriptures. Underline the ways that Christ is superior. Highlight His authority.

Hebrews 1: 1-4

Ephesians 1: 18-23

We recognize human authority. Well, most of us do. Have you seen those videos of people being disrespectful or even antagonistic to police officers? Most of the time, the police officer responds calmly but if the situation escalates, the offender spends at least some time behind bars. I have worked in places where I had tremendous respect for my supervisors as godly people–kind men and women who cared deeply for others and made decisions that they believed to be consistent with scripture. Others I didn't necessarily agree with their decisions but liked them based on personality. Others made decisions that I felt were wrong and did so with a surly attitude. But, in all cases, as scripture requires (Romans 13: 1-7), I respected their position of authority. In respecting and submitting to God, there are no personality conflicts, no bad decisions, no mistakes at all. If we respect human authority, then we surely can respect and submit to our loving and just God's supreme authority.

SUBMIT AND COMMIT TO HIM

We make a choice once (to clarify-we only are saved one time. As my husband would say, "It's a done deal.") to accept Him as Savior. The choice to be fully committed to Him is made moment by moment.

As you reread each scripture above (Hebrews 1:1-4 and Ephesians 1:18-23), pray about ways that you need to submit and commit to Him.

Read Proverbs 3:5-7

A few years ago, my husband was involved in an accident caused by a drunk driver. He had multiple injuries, including a large cut from the base of his skull to the bottom of his chin, broken vertebrae, crushed nose, separated sternum, broken ribs, and various scrapes. During tirage, the doctors also discovered that he had a tumor in his kidney. All this added to the ongoing consequences of severe diabetes. A year of surgeries for treatment of cancer and repair of injuries followed. He had issues with anxiety, panic, and sleeplessness.

Many of the people in the church where he pastored were very supportive of him, but the stress of his multiple health concerns and of dealing with the issues a pastor must address was too much for him. He resigned with the plan to take his long-term disability insurance. I was to find a job while he took over some of the things I had been doing: homeschooling our son, laundry, cooking, cleaning, paying bills, yard work, etc. We put our house on the market and moved to the small cabin we had built years before. We bought a few chickens, ducks, turkeys, rabbits and goats and set out to live a simpler life.

Many other things that we thought would work out have not. Truth be told, from a human perspective, we are a pretty good example of "Murphy's Law." (Various) Our poultry shelters collapsed under an ice storm. The goats refused to stay in the fence. They preferred to butt their heads into the storm doors, eat my potted plants and shrubs, and make themselves at home on my patio furniture. (I won't be specific about what they did on the furniture, but I had to power wash it frequently.) A snake ate the baby rabbits. The adult rabbits ran away when the goats knocked over their hutches. When our house didn't sell within a reasonable time, we used a reputable management company to lease it. The renter they found was a nightmare to the neighborhood and to us. The rental agent was afraid to address the issues with him because of his temper. Eventually he left of his own accord under cover of darkness. We were then able to make repairs and list the property again. Ultimately, our house did not sell for over seven years. My husband continued to have health issues. I won't go into greater detail of our comedy of errors. The point is, trusting in the Lord and not trying to figure things out by our own understanding can be difficult.

Accepting that "making my paths straight" did not necessarily mean what I thought it should mean has been a journey for me. I have cried, been angry at my husband, wondered what God is trying to teach us or why He is disciplining us, etc. I have even thought, briefly, because I know this is not the truth, that God must hate me. Submitting to His ways is not always easy, but He is always right.

What are some circumstances when you have struggled, or continue to struggle with trusting God and not depending on your own understanding? How has God's definition of "making your paths straight" been different from yours?

GOD'S LOVING DISCIPLINE

Read Hebrews 12:8-10

We have five children, and each of them responded differently to discipline. The oldest would argue. Her most frequent response was "I don't know what you're talking about." The second was easier. My husband could clear his throat, or I could look at him over the top of my glasses and he would stop what he was doing. The third could lie with amazing believability. The fourth was an eye roller, as if our discipline was the most ridiculous thing she had ever heard of. The fifth was angry with us for trying to discipline him. As Christians, how do we respond to God's discipline? Do we submit? Do we argue? Do we lie to God (as if that were even possible) and make excuses? Do we count His discipline as a joke? Do we become angry with Him?

What is your response to God's discipline?

HUMBLE OURSELVES

Read James 4:6-8

I'm reminded of the song by Mac Davis that says, "It's hard to be humble when you're perfect in every way." (Davis) The song was written, as I understand it, to be funny, but it gives us food for thought in light of the scripture. I have a yearly evaluation at my job. Part of the process is that I must rate myself in several areas. My principal also rates me by the same criteria. Then we are to work together to develop a personal growth plan. I am not good at this process. I will either focus entirely on my weaknesses, and give myself unacceptable or basic ratings, or I will take the prideful route and see myself as distinguished in all areas. Neither is correct. For Christians the right way to see ourselves is as a vessel of Christ. On our own, we are unacceptable. But, when in humility, we submit to God, He will use us. He will draw near to us, cleanse us and equip us for the work he has for us.

Reflect on your own struggles with pride or worthlessness. Take a moment to draw near to God, submitting yourself to Him.

HAVE NO IDOLS

Read 1 Samuel 7:3

We tend to look at this scripture, and others like it, and think it doesn't apply to us because we don't pray to golden statues. But what is an idol? Anything that has more importance to us than God, or anything that holds unmerited value to us. I am a pretty sentimental person. Things remind me of people. A candy dish given as a Christmas present by one of my Sunday School students reminds me of that young lady. I never knew my grandmother, but her pump organ means a lot to me. A tea pitcher reminds me of my childhood. You get the idea. My daughter calls me a hoarder, but I wouldn't go quite that far. When we moved to our cabin, almost all of our possessions were placed in storage. This was a struggle for me, because at a time when my world had been turned upside down, things that gave me comfort were no longer within my reach. I didn't worship these things, but they had significant value to me. I know that my comfort is in God, not earthly possessions, so this was a way God led me to understand that idolatry is more than my superficial understanding.

What idols do you have?

TURN OUR HEARTS TOWARD HIM

Read 1 Kings 8: 57-61

Solomon prayed this prayer at the dedication of the temple. As the Holy Spirit speaks to you through the scripture, He will reveal things to you. Take a minute to look prayerfully at these verses again.

How does God speak to you through Solomon's prayer?

As I look at these scriptures, this is how they speak to me. Verse 58 says "May He turn our hearts to Him…" This reminds me that my walk with God is not based on my own efforts, but rather on submission to God. He is the One who can turn my heart to Himself. Verse 60 says "so that all the people of the earth may know that the Lord is God…" Our commitment to God and His work in our lives is a testimony to those around us. One of my previous jobs was assistant administrator at a children's rehabilitation facility. Often people would come to my office and begin their conversation with this statement, "I know you are a religious person, so I was wondering what you thought about…" Now, that is one of my pet peeves. I am not religious. I have a relationship with Jesus Christ. I don't know what they saw in me that made them come to me for advice, but it gave me an opportunity to explain to them about my relationship with Christ. People around you see who you are, not just what you say and do. You are either a positive or negative testimony for Jesus. God uses our commitment to Him so that others may know Him too. Verse 61 says "And may your hearts be fully committed to the Lord our God…" Once again, I am struck with the complete commitment that God expects. Solomon doesn't just say for the people to be committed to God; he says fully committed. The question I must ask myself, and the question you must ask yourself, is: Are you committed to Christ or are you **fully** committed to Him?

THE DESIRES OF OUR HEARTS

Read Psalm 37: 3-7

I love God's Word, and particularly the Psalms. Practically every word in these verses touches my heart. I am sitting on my back porch right now, looking across the pasture on the farm where we live. My great-great grandfather homesteaded this land. The place where my animals pasture now has pastured animals or produced crops for my family for over a century and a half. I find my view to be very peaceful.

Look at verse 3. When we trust in God, and do what He leads us to do, we dwell in the land and enjoy safe pastures. Even though some things have gone comically (or tragically) wrong since God has "turned our world upside down," He has blessed us in so many ways. I have a job that I truly enjoy. We have food to eat. The bills are paid, even if I do "lean to my own understanding" sometimes and stress about it. We have wonderful neighbors in an extended rural community. Our son, daughter in love, and grandkids live near enough to visit often. Our other adult children and grandchildren are closer now than they were. My husband is able to preach at a small church near our home without the stress of where we were when his accident occurred. And most importantly, God has given me a peace that even when I don't understand His plan, it is always for my good and His glory.

Think about your own circumstances. How do you see that your obedience to God has let you dwell in safe pastures? Perhaps, your pastures don't feel so safe because you have not trusted God. Confess that to God and ask His forgiveness. Ask Him to help you trust Him.

Verse four says "take delight in the Lord, and He will give you the desires of your heart." Sometimes we only look at the second half of that statement. We want Him to give us the desires of our hearts, even when our delight is not in Him. That is not what the scripture says. If our hearts delight in

Him, then our desires will be His desires. There are lots of things that I may desire that do not reflect my delight being placed in God. I desire new cabinet tops, or even a new house, but those things are not based on a heart focused on God. Those are earthly pleasures. Several years ago, I completed a life changing study <u>Experiencing God</u> by Henry Blackaby (Henry Blackaby). He said, "Let your hearts be broken by the things that break the heart of God." Wow! Blackaby's statement still leaves me speechless. If my delight is in God, then I desire the things He desires. How do we know the things He desires? An obvious answer is to read the scriptures and see the things He specifically tells us that He desires. Just briefly, He wants people to be saved. He wants us to grow in our relationship with Him. He wants us to love others. He wants us to have fellowship with Him and with our Christian brothers and sisters. He wants us to be sincerely, completely, wholeheartedly committed to Him.

Do you desire the things that God desires? What are some things that you feel God has laid on your heart that He desires for or through you?

Reread verses six and seven. My principal was a godly man. He put scripture verses in our mailboxes. He started faculty meetings with prayer. He showed genuine compassion to the students and staff. What seemed to me to be quite suddenly, we learned that his contract had not been renewed. I don't know exactly what happened. I only know the gossip, and we all know what scripture says about gossip. (The gossip does not say that he did anything unethical, immoral, or illegal.) But I do know that his response to the situation only served to increase my respect for him. He never said anything to discredit others. He sent us all an email telling us goodbye. He talked about how he wasn't sure what God's plan for him had been when he was hired, how he felt God had used him at our school, and expressed anticipation for where God would lead him next. In my eyes, his righteousness and vindication shine through this situation.

Can you think of a situation when God has used difficult situations to let righteousness shine?

CHOOSE TO SERVE GOD

Read Joshua 24:19-24

Joshua's statement "You are not able to serve the Lord" is profound. We are not capable of serving the Lord if our service is done only by our own efforts. Look at the rest of this passage. God asks us to put away the things that are a hindrance to serving Him and to yield to Him. Yield to Him. This is the way that we are able to serve Him.

Yielding can be difficult, and even stressful. We live in the country now, where there is very little traffic. But we have lived in populated areas with lots of traffic. One of the most stressful parts of driving in the city is merging into traffic on the Interstate at rush hour. My heart races as I steel my nerves on the entrance ramp, and I breathe a sigh of relief when I make it safely into the flow of traffic. Yielding to traffic is frightening. In the same way, when we are comfortable with the spiritual status quo, the decision to yield to God can be frightening. But the only way to reach my destination in traffic is to yield to traffic and continue my journey. The only way to continue our journey of spiritual growth is to yield completely to God.

Be honest. Do you have any fears about yielding: totally, fully, completely, to God? What fears do you have?

Read Joshua 24:15

Some states have "Right to Work" laws. By and large, people are not compelled to work at a specific job. We choose where we want to apply for a job. We choose which "master" we serve. We also make a choice to serve God or to serve false gods, whatever those may be. Think about the things that we choose to give priority in our lives. Can these things be your god? Education, money, family, friendships, recreation, social media, knowledge of current events, politics, organizations, hobbies? And one that requires some soul searching is "Do I place church activities over relationship with God?"

What false gods are you tempted to choose to serve? Ask for forgiveness now and resolve to choose to serve God.

Read Deuteronomy 30:11-20

As part of my professional development, I recently attended a workshop on how to conduct a Functional Behavior Assessment and develop a Behavior Improvement Plan for children who have a pattern of frequent inappropriate or unacceptable behavior. Let that sink in a minute. Do you think that God sees us as having a pattern of frequent inappropriate or unacceptable behavior? I know He does for me. Since the workshop was fresh on my mind, I read the scripture above and thought that this looks very much like a Behavior Improvement Plan for us.

Reread the scripture, looking for

1. *Causes of our unacceptable behavior*
2. *What unacceptable behavior we have*

3. *The acceptable behavior God expects from us*
4. *Negative consequences of our unacceptable behavior*
5. *Positive consequences of acceptable behavior*

FOR THE SAKE OF HIS NAME

Read Psalm 25:11-13

Often, I hear myself praying something like this. "Lord, please don't let ____ (the sinful or embarrassing thing I said or did) push others away from you. Forgive me for doing something that reflects poorly on You. Don't let my sinfulness keep others from coming to You." Look at verse 11. "For the sake of your name, Lord…" There is an old country song by Cal Smith that talks about "…you self-righteous woman". (Smith) Another by Johnny Cash says, "You're so heavenly minded, you're no earthly good." (Cash) Now, please don't get your theology from country music because there is some pretty strange theology (heresy) in country music, but, just for a minute, think about how the lost world views us as Christians. Do those around us see a shallowness that results in words and actions which are religious in nature but clearly do not reflect God's heart toward our fellow citizens of earth?

How then can we avoid saying and doing things that do not testify accurately who God is in our lives? Look at verse 12. It's a heart thing. Where are our hearts? Do we "fear" the Lord? What does it mean to fear the Lord? While many sermons could be preached on that one question, let us simplify for our purposes. Fearing God is recognizing who He is. An oversimplification would say a healthy respect for His authority. But, in that aspect, I fear policemen and my supervisor at work but that in no way compares with God's authority. The song "Above All" by Michael W. Smith says, "There's no way to measure what You're worth.' The words to this song help us to understand the fear of the Lord. This fear of the Lord is the only way we can live a life that reflects God to others. God will instruct us in the ways we should choose.

BE CONSECRATED

consecrate (verb) *[with obj.]* make or declare (something, typically a church) sacred; dedicate formally to a religious or divine purpose: *informal* devote (something) exclusively to a particular purpose: (New Oxford Dictionary)

Scripture is clear that we must be willing to rid ourselves of that which is sinful. The definition above for "consecrate" doesn't really address a personal consecration to God, but the principle applies.

Look at the following scriptures when God asked His people to consecrate themselves.

Read Exodus 19: 10-23

The Israelites were required to consecrate themselves from everything unholy and were still not allowed to approach God when He appeared on Mount Sinai. Moses would soon receive the Law, which prescribed the regulations, sacrifices, and feasts, which God put in place to teach the Israelites about Himself, to make them aware of their own sinfulness, and to allow them to praise and worship Him. But we have Jesus, the fulfillment of the Law and the once for all time Sacrifice for our sin. We are told to approach God with confidence because of the sacrifice that Jesus made for us.

Read Hebrews 4:16

Our consecration is built on the foundation of our salvation experience, our accepting the gift of forgiveness through Jesus' death, burial, and resurrection. We receive His Spirit. We forever belong to Him. Our continuing consecration is based on an ongoing confession of our sins. One Sunday morning (I don't know what I was thinking), I gave our 2-year-old son a bath and dressed him for church before, yes, before, giving him his oatmeal for breakfast. His bib shielded his good clothes, but he turned the full oatmeal bowl upside down on his head like it was a hat. He was clean, but he needed to have his hair washed before he was ready to go to church. David, a man after God's own heart said, "If I harbor sin in my heart, God will not hear me." (Psalm 66: 18) John tells us that if we confess our sins, God will be faithful to cleanse us. (1 John 1: 9-10). We are consecrated by Jesus' blood, but we continue to be consecrated by His forgiveness as we confess our sins. Unlike the Israelites, our consecration is not by human effort. We can approach God with confidence because of His mercy and forgiveness.

Read Leviticus 20:7-8

God tells the Israelites (and us) to consecrate ourselves, but He doesn't leave us wondering how to do that. He tells us that He is the One who makes us holy. The reason we need to be holy is because He is holy. When we keep and follow His decrees, he will make us holy. Is there a difference between "keeping" His decrees and "following" His decrees?

Many of us surf the web these days. When we find something that is particularly significant or meaningful to us, we click that little star (or whatever your icon is on your computer) and add that site to our favorites. We keep it. My car has a navigation system. I enter an address, or a point of interest and those directions guide me to where I need to be. The navigation system also allows me to add a specific number of favorites so that I can easily return to those places from anywhere. I keep those addresses. Those things that have more value to me are kept. Others are used briefly and put aside. Keeping God's decrees means that they have significance to us. Then, there is another level of "following" on social media. If we really feel like a particular person or organization provides important or interesting information, we will "follow" them. We are interested in what they have to say. We want to be aware of what they are doing, thinking and feeling. When we keep God's decrees and follow them, we consider Him most significant and want to know His thoughts, actions and emotions.

Read Joshua 3:5

Amazing things! Who doesn't want to experience amazing things? And what a reason to consecrate ourselves! God can do more amazing things than any theme park creator, movie producer, or sports team. At my ten-year class reunion, my classmates were asked to share the most amazing/significant thing they had experienced in the ten years since we graduated. One classmate said that her amazing experience was being present when her favorite college sports team won the national championship. At that time, and to this day, that saddens me. The most amazing things we experience are those times that God reveals Himself to us in whatever ways He chooses. We had a Labrador retriever who was probably the smartest dog we have ever had. Multiple times he made us aware of threatening situations we would otherwise have missed. He was trained to lie quietly by the back door. From a purely human perspective, he was pretty amazing. But one morning as I had my quiet time, the dog was, as usual, lying by the back door. It was one of those times when I could truly feel that God was present. Then suddenly the dog began to, the best way I can describe it is, to sing praises. It was a combination of barking and howling. He had never done that before and did not again. How amazing that when God is present, even the animals praise Him!

What are some amazing things you have seen God do?

With God's miraculous power, and Joshua's leadership, the Israelites had conquered Jericho by walking around the wall. God had caused the walls to fall in. He had commanded the people to destroy everything. Achan had disobeyed God's command and taken some valuable items from Babylonia and hidden them. When they next went to battle against Ai, they were defeated. They didn't understand why. Then God answered their question.

Read Joshua 7:12-13

God described these items of plunder taken from Jericho as "devoted to destruction." The entire nation of Israel had experienced defeat because one man disobeyed God by taking a beautiful robe, two hundred shekels of silver and a bar of gold weighing fifty shekels. I don't know how the value of the items he took would translate into our monetary system, but I am certain it wasn't worth the lives of 36 men.

Why do you think it was so important that the plunder be destroyed?

God tells Joshua that the Israelites will not be able to defeat their enemies unless they consecrate themselves and get rid of the things that He has commanded them to destroy. Our son has been deployed four times, once to Iraq and three times to Afghanistan. He knows much better than I do what it means to face an enemy. Christians in some areas of the world today are imprisoned, and even martyred for their faith. That is definitely facing an enemy. The closest thing I have experienced with human "enemies" are mild annoyances compared to real enemies. But the greatest enemies that any of us face are spiritual enemies. In our spiritual battles, there are things that hinder our victory. We have treasures that we think we are hiding from God that keeps us from defeating our enemy.

What plunder are you hiding that God has devoted to destruction? Are you willing to get rid of it?

STAND FIRM

Read 1 Peter 5:8-9

The devil is our enemy. He is <u>like</u> a roaring lion. Jesus IS the Lion of Judah. (Read Revelation 5:5) The devil is merely an imitation. Jesus' purpose is to save us and give us victory. The devil's purpose is to devour and defeat us. Peter tells us to resist him. The only way to resist the devil is to stand firm in our faith in the true Lion, Jesus Christ our Savior. How can we stand firm? Surely not in our own power. We stand firm in His power.

Read Ephesians 5: 10-17

List the ways Paul tells the Ephesians to prepare for battle against spiritual enemies.

STEADFAST

steadfast (adjective) resolutely or dutifully firm and unwavering: *steadfast loyalty.* (New Oxford Dictionary)

What attitude must we have in order to have a steadfast spirit within us?

Read Psalm 51:7-10

Psalm 51 was one of my daddy's favorite scriptures. I never read it without thinking of him, and for several reasons. He wasn't a perfect man. He would be the first one to tell you that. For as long as I can remember, if he ever talked about his funeral, he would say that he didn't want the preacher to talk about how good he was, because everyone would know he was lying. He did ask that the plan of salvation be presented at his funeral, and my husband did a wonderful job with that. One of the things I admire about my daddy was his willingness to acknowledge his sinfulness. Because of that, he walked steadfastly with his Lord. A precursor to steadfastness is repentance and acknowledgement of our sin. We repent. God gives us a steadfast spirit.

David was hiding in a cave because Saul was pursuing him to kill him. Yet he is able to say that his heart is steadfast.

Read Psalm 57:4-7

Look closely at these verses. What reasons does David give that his heart is steadfast?

At first glance, we see that those who pursued him have fallen into their own pit. But look at verse 5. God is exalted and his glory is over all the earth. The pursuers fell into the pit, not because of their own clumsiness, but because God is exalted, and His glory fills the earth. When we face adversity, the key to steadfastness is to recognize and acknowledge God's glory and exalt Him in our lives. It's a horse before the cart type thing. David's heart was steadfast in his trust in God. His trust was not dependent on the defeat of his enemies. His enemies' defeat was the result of his steadfast faith in God.

HE IS WORTHY OF PRAISE

Read Psalm 108:1-5

How did David promise to worship God? Why is he worshiping God?

David worshiped with all his soul. He sang. He made music. He began his praise at dawn. He is praised among the nations and among the peoples. The reason for his enthusiastic and public worship was God's great love, His faithfulness, and His glory.

I'm not a gifted musician, but I'm not completely deaf. Honestly, I have heard some special music sung at church that made my ears hurt. Be honest. You have too. And I have heard professional grade performances as well. Neither of those things are important. David's worship came from a steadfast heart. While I am assuming that David was, indeed, a gifted musician both in instrument and in voice, the thing that made his worship pleasing to God was his steadfast heart.

Pray now in worship and praise as you reread the sentiments of this psalm in song.

Read Psalm 119:1-7

Notice that the writer of this psalm longs for this but feels shame because he feels like he does not live up to God's expectations. He looks at others and sees them seemingly walking blameless, keeping His statutes, and seeking Him wholeheartedly. He bemoans his own inability to do so, and longs to serve Him.

Apply this psalmist's struggle with your own life. What do you learn from his words?

I know that comparing myself with others is futile. We don't truly know a person's heart. And others don't know our hearts. Only God knows a person's heart. I may look at someone and think they have it all together, when they may be overwhelmed with questions, failures, and heartaches. The way others see us doesn't matter. The psalmist expresses a pure, passionate desire to learn God's way and be upright in heart.

We have talked about definitions that explain the concepts related to a wholehearted commitment to God. We have looked at scriptures that tell us why consecration is important and the results of not following God completely. Let's look next at the results of surrendering our lives wholly to Him.

CHAPTER 2

WHOLEHEARTED EVIDENCE

What is the evidence of wholehearted commitment to God in our daily lives?

Colossians 1:3-8 New International Version (NIV) 3 We always thank God, the Father of our Lord Jesus Christ, when we pray for you, 4 because we have heard of your faith in Christ Jesus and of the love you have for all God's people— 5 the faith and love that spring from the hope stored up for you in heaven and about which you have already heard in the true message of the gospel 6 that has come to you. In the same way, the gospel is bearing fruit and growing throughout the whole world—just as it has been doing among you since the day you heard it and truly understood God's grace. 7 You learned it from Epaphras, our dear fellow servant, who is a faithful minister of Christ on our behalf, 8 and who also told us of your love in the Spirit.

List evidence of wholehearted devotion to God that Paul describes in the Christians in Colossae.

OTHERS WILL SEE EVIDENCE OF CHRIST IN OUR LIVES

RADIANCE

Read Exodus 34:29-35

A young woman would periodically sing special music at church. When she did, her face was radiant. It was clear to see that her song was truly an act of worship, and not a performance. I wanted her to know how much I appreciated her genuine heart for worship. I told her, "You look like Moses when you sing." I think I hurt her feelings until I explained what I meant. I want to look like Moses. How about you?

Why was Moses' face radiant? How does that apply to us?

Read Psalm 34:4-5

How does David describe the source of radiance?

The source of radiance is the joy that results from seeking the Lord completely, looking to Him to answer us, deliver us and protect us from all the dangers we face.

We spend money on all kinds of products and services to help us look younger, prettier, more attractive. We may even use the word "radiant" to describe the outcome. But true beauty, true radiance, is not based on what we put on the outside, but on Who dwells on the inside.

FAITH

Read Matthew 8: 5-13

The centurion stated the situation, that his servant was paralyzed and suffering. Then, Jesus asked if he wanted Him to come heal the servant. Reflecting on some of my own prayers, and remembering prayer requests at church, I see a pattern of us telling God what we think He should do about a given situation. Heal my aunt. Give me that job. Let me marry this person. Of course, we want to use good manners, so we say "please, Lord…" Sound familiar?

How does this habit of prayer reflect our trust or lack of trust in God's wisdom and unfailing love?

How did the centurion's recognition of Jesus' authority affect his faith?

Read Matthew 9: 2-7

These men brought their friend to Jesus. Again, scripture does not state that they made a specific request of Jesus, only that Jesus saw their faith. Jesus did not mention healing him, but instead told the man that his sins were forgiven. While we do not know the response of the men who brought him, we know that the teachers of the law accused Jesus of blasphemy. In response, Jesus asked them which was easier, to forgive sins or to heal.

Which do you think is easier, to forgive sins or to heal?

Think about the prayer requests made in your Sunday School class or prayer meetings. Most that I hear are for those who are sick or bereaved. Sadly, I also wonder if people's prayer requests are simply attention seeking. My daughter was a Jr. High student at a wonderful Christian School. The teachers regularly asked the students for prayer requests and prayed before classes began. One day at a football game her teacher approached me and told me that she was praying for our youngest son, who was an infant at the time. I had no idea what she was talking about. When I asked our daughter about it, she admitted to requesting prayer for him because the other students had prayer requests, and she felt left out. She told her class that he was very sick with a life-threatening condition. While I was upset with her, I wonder if we as adults do the same thing, not really expressing genuine concern for others, but simply wanting to feel like we are part of the group.

Very seldom do I hear anyone request prayer that someone be saved. Either people are ashamed to pray for their lost loved ones, so they have an "unspoken" request, or they are not truly concerned for the lost. Or they lack faith that God will answer. Our church was planning a series of revival meetings. Before this event, people made prayer requests for various people to be saved. One request was for an elderly man whose wife attended. One deacon responded, "It won't do any good. We have prayed for him for 30 years and nothing has happened." Do you know what happened? That man was saved during the revival.

On the other hand, for me personally, it seems easier to trust that God is not willing that any should perish, but that all should come to repentance than to believe that He will disrupt the course of a fatal disease. I feel much more comfortable praying for my lost family members to be saved than I do for someone to be healed.

Over the span of several years, God taught me a lesson, even though I am not fully sure I understand the whole of what He was showing me. When I was a junior in college, my mother was diagnosed with breast cancer. The doctor said that it had spread to her lymph nodes and that she had a 30% chance of survival. I prayed fervently that God would heal her, and He did. Fifteen years later, she was diagnosed with pancreatic cancer. I wanted to pray that she would be healed. I knew God was capable of doing so, because He had done so before. But in my heart and spirit, for some reason, I knew that He was not giving me the freedom to pray for her healing. She died six months later. I knew it was God's plan for her. Up to this point, I felt like God was teaching me a very clear lesson: He would let me know when and if it was in His will to pray for healing. Several years after that, a dear sister in Christ had a recurrence of cancer. The cancer had spread to various parts of her body. I prayed, and I felt like God had clearly led me to the scripture that said this illness will not end in death.

- **John 11:4 New International Version (NIV) 4** When he heard this, Jesus said, "This sickness will not end in death. No, it is for God's glory so that God's Son may be glorified through it."

I prayed with full confidence that God would heal her. Even when others were saying that she wasn't going to live, I was adamant that she would be healed, or at the very least go into remission. She died. My heart was broken, and I was confused. I absolutely know He was teaching me something, but it is not clear enough to me even now to put into words.

What lessons do you learn from my short testimony here?

Which healing is more important and more significant, physical, emotional or spiritual?

Read Matthew 9: 18-26

We see in this passage two examples of extreme faith. The synagogue leader said, "My daughter is dead, but You can make her alive." And, the woman said, "If I can just touch Him, I will be healed." I want to have that much faith. Honestly, I don't think I have that strong a faith, but I want to have.

Read Matthew 9: 27-31

Jesus healed these men according to their faith. Often, I am struck by the seeming futility of our traditional Wednesday night prayer meetings. We ask for requests and several names are called. We pray through that list of names, if we remember who they are, or if we wrote them down. Then we go home and watch television or some other meaningless activity. What if God answered our prayers according to our faith? Would any of our prayers be answered? But these men truly believed, miraculously received their sight, and went around everywhere telling others what Jesus had done for them.

Once a friend asked me to be part of a quilting prayer group. I didn't know how to quilt, but was excited to learn. We would quilt in the morning, eat lunch, then have a prayer time. I was always amazed by how one of the ladies prayed. She never asked God to do anything. She prayed prayers of thanksgiving for what He was going to do. "Thank you, Lord for healing my friend. Thank you, Lord for convicting her husband so that he can be saved…"

Read Matthew 15: 21-28

Jesus often used a process to teach His disciples a lesson. Notice that the Canaanite woman was crying out, simply stating her need and asking for Jesus' help. Jesus seemingly ignored her to the point that she became quite annoying to the disciples. They asked Him to send her away. Why hadn't they sent her away? Maybe they had tried but she was so persistent that their efforts were to no avail. I don't know. Jesus makes the interesting statement that He was sent only to the people of

Israel. It seems that He was speaking to her, rather than responding to His disciples, because she then approached Him in response to His statement. He responded again, this time with a metaphor about bread and dogs. Look at her response. Was she arguing with what He said? She certainly responded to what He said in a way that showed great faith. I think she also showed great courage to speak with Him so boldly. Is my faith strong enough to give me courage to speak boldly? Jesus complimented her great faith and granted her request. Since we know He is all knowing, He knew the whole sequence of events and conversation before it unfolded before the disciples' eyes. This series of interactions was there to teach the disciples, and us, a lesson.

What do you learn from this conversation?

Read Romans 1:8

The faith of the Christians in Rome was well known. Sadly, in our world today, we hear of Christian brothers and sisters who are brutally tortured and martyred because they refuse to renounce their faith in Jesus. Their faith is being reported all over the world, literally. But in our churches and communities, very little is said about our faith. Why is that? Where is <u>our</u> wholehearted faith in Christ?

Why do you think our faith, yours and mine, aren't being talked about in our communities?

Read Ephesians 1:15-21

According to tradition, Paul was in prison in Rome when he wrote his letter to the Ephesians. He was either remembering or had received word of their faith that was paired with their love for all fellow believers. Paul was praying for their continued spiritual growth. Even in those whose faith is recognized by others, and is well known, continued growth is necessary. We cannot become complacent in our walk with God.

Look again at Ephesians 1: 15-21. List or underline ways that Paul prayed that the Ephesians would grow in their faith.

Read Revelation 2:1-7

What admonition did Jesus have for the church at Ephesus?

Contrast Paul's thankfulness and prayers for the Ephesian church with Jesus' message to them in the Revelation.

Our decision for a wholehearted faith happens daily, moment by moment. The faith of the people in Ephesus was known all over the world when Paul wrote to them, but something happened between then and the time that Jesus spoke through John in the Revelation. We must daily renew our love for Him, as we exhibit faith and obedience.

Read 1 Thessalonians 1:3-10

In his letter to the church in Thessalonica, Paul lists several characteristics that are evident because of their faith.

Look through 1 Thessalonians 1: 3-10 again. List or underline how the Thessalonians demonstrated their faith.

Read Philemon 1:4-6

As we look back over the letters Paul wrote to the churches, we see that faith is directly related to their spiritual growth and to their actions. He writes of the actions prompted by faith in the Thessalonians. He prays that the Ephesians will grow spiritually and that Philemon's faith may be effective in deepening his understanding. Our faith in Jesus as Lord is central to our actions and our understanding. Our actions have no merit without faith. Conversely, when we have faith, our faith will result in, as James says, works. Works do not save us, but are a direct result of faith. Likewise, we cannot become mature Christians without a growing faith.

Read James 2: 14-18.

UNITY IN THE FAITH

Read Ephesians 4:11-13

My husband does not like church business meetings. His pastor's heart wants to spend that time in studying the Bible rather than face the possibility of a conflict over some small matter of business. On the other hand, when I was a child, I always looked forward to the monthly business meetings for that same reason. It was always interesting to me to see the adults around me passionately argue about whether we should have paper or cloth doilies under the punch bowl, or some other matter of similar significance. (It is also sad to say that business meetings were one of the most interesting and exciting things I remember about church as a child. That is an entirely different discussion.) As humans we will always have different preferences about doilies, carpet or paint color, or what time services should begin, but as Christians we must desire a unity in the faith. Knowledge of Jesus, maturity, and the fullness of Christ are closely tied to unity in our faith, building up the body of Christ and serving others. Unity in the faith is much more than agreeing about doilies: Unity is a result of spiritual maturity and a wholehearted yielding to Christ's work in our lives.

Read 3 John 2-4.

Our faith brings joy to those who have had a part in our spiritual growth. And we find joy in seeing continued growth in those He has allowed us to nurture in their faith. Four young ladies came to my house weekly for Bible study and encouragement in dealing with various addictions and traumas in their lives. I would like to say that they all continue to walk with Christ. However, one stole some items from my home which had both sentimental and monetary value. (I didn't confront her because I had no proof and didn't want to break that relationship.) Spending time with her was the most emotionally and spiritually draining thing I have ever done. That spiritual battle was lost, for whatever reason, and she returned to her former lifestyle. Looking back, I doubt that there was ever any sincerity in her. I don't know where she is now. Perhaps God has continued to convict her and has miraculously brought her genuinely to Himself. Another had so damaged her brain with drugs that I don't know if she was even capable of comprehending what we discussed. Certainly, her contribution to the discussion didn't make much sense. She was brutally murdered, stabbed multiple times in an apparent drug related situation. These situations do not bring me joy, other than in knowing that I was obedient to God in trying .to bring them to Him. But the other two ladies bring me great joy. I seldom see either of them, but I know that both continue to serve God faithfully. And one has a part of my heart that defies description. Just the thought of her brings tears of joy to my eyes. She is married now and has five children. She has also adopted a child with Down syndrome and two children who test HIV positive. She actively teaches her children and other children of the love of God. When I see this amazing person and remember the depths from which God lifted her, my joy overflows.

LOVE

Our love for God must be greater than our love for anyone or anything else. This week at Children's Mini Camp, I taught the children the song "I Am My Beloved's and He is Mine." This scripture comes from the Song of Solomon. The lesson I wanted them to learn is that our love for God and His for us is superior to any other.

The story of Abraham and Isaac on the mountain is a difficult passage to read. Read it prayerfully.

Read Genesis 22 :1-19

Notice that God calls Isaac the "son that you love." I think this has such great significance. My second child was an easy baby. He slept like a rock. Even his older sister screaming into his bassinet didn't wake him. When he was awake, he seldom cried. I loved him so much, not more than the others, but he was just easier. If you are a parent of multiple children, you understand this. (On a personal note, to my children and grandchildren, when and if they read this, I have never loved one of you more than the others. I love you all with all my heart.) One day I was holding him, and God convicted me. I didn't hear His voice, but I know as surely as I know anything that He asked me this question, "Do you love him more than you love Me?" Tears began to flow down my cheeks, because I knew the answer to that question at that moment of time was that I did. I took him in my hands, the way that only a tiny infant can be held, and lifted him up toward heaven. "Lord, he is Yours to take if he is more important to me than You are." God did not take him from me. He gave him back to me. But from that moment forward, I saw him differently. No, he isn't a great pastor or evangelist, but God has guided his life in marvelous ways. I will never forget the lesson that God taught me that day. My love for Him must be the greatest love in my life.

Read Song of Songs 6:3a

When He really is our Beloved, then our love for others becomes purer, more sincere, more sacrificial, and more unconditional.

Read 1 John 4:7-8

Read John 13:34-36

Jesus commands us to love others as He loved us. Three things stand out here. He commands-not suggests, not asks-but He <u>commands</u> us to love others in the same way He loves us. I'm not a Greek language scholar, but I have heard others teach that when Jesus asked Peter three times if he loved Him, He used the Greek word "agape" in the first two questions, and "phileo" in the third question. Jesus' intent is that we love with a God-like love. Not simply a brotherly love, but a godly love. This love for our brothers and sisters is a testimony to others that we are truly His disciples. When I ask myself if I have this type of love for others, my honest answer would be that I don't. I really like food, particularly things deep fried. For the first 20+ years of my life, French fries were my staple food. When we were newlyweds, we ate supper one night with my parents, who cooked steak and French fries. Wanting to save the best for last, I ate my French fries sparingly so that I could savor them at the end of my meal. My husband wolfed down his and had steak left with no French fries to go with them. Poor planning on his part, I would say. My mother asked him if he wanted some of my fries. That put me in an awkward situation, because I obviously did not love him enough to give him my fries. I asked him if he wanted them, hoping against hope that he would love me enough to realize he shouldn't take them. When he said that he did want them, I was forced to tell him he couldn't have them. He still reminds me of this often. The point here is that we are by nature self-centered. Even with those we love the most, we do not love sacrificially in even the small, insignificant things. So, if we ask ourselves if we love sacrificially in matters of even greater significance, the answer is probably not.

Search your own heart. Do you love sacrificially?

Read 1 Thessalonians 1:3

I had a professor in college who was truly an inspiration to me. God's grace brought her from a life of poverty on a Navajo Reservation, from being labeled as unable to learn, from a religion with questionable theology to true salvation through the sacrifice Jesus made for us. Because of His work in her life, she was accepted into a major university at the age of 14, obtained advanced degrees from a prestigious university and then to a teaching position at a well-respected Christian university where I met her. I took every class that she taught, not because I was required to, but because of the lessons I learned from her, both academically and personally. She had as many as 20 troubled children and teens in her home at a time. I spent some time in her home with her and these children. Their stories were horrendous. Their responses to their situations often resulted in bizarre behaviors and psychiatric diagnoses. I will always remember this statement she made. "Sometimes what we see in children are not abnormal behaviors, but normal reactions to abnormal situations." My time under her tutelage has forever colored my response to the children God places in my path. She received no monetary profit for the sacrifices she made for the children and for her college students. She ministered to them and to us because of her great love for her Savior. Her labor was prompted by love. Whatever ministry God leads us to do, our labor should be prompted by love.

Does love prompt the service and ministry in which you are involved or is there some other motivation?

Read 1 Thessalonians 3:6

While my husband was able to pastor full time, we lived and ministered in four states and several churches. We also participated in various mission trips in other states and on other continents. In each of those places I have pleasant memories. Thanks to social media, I now have contact with people I haven't seen in years. These people were not always what you would call close friends. But I remember their faith in God and their love for Him and for us. Periodically we communicate through social media, and consistently we will each invite the other to visit, because we would love to see each other. An expression of God's love in the lives of His children transcends time and distance. We long to see other believers.

When my husband was in seminary, he pastored a wonderful country church. We were only there for about a year and a half. Our last Sunday there, one of the teenage girls sang the song "Friends are Friends Forever" (M. Smith) by Michael W. Smith as special music. It made me cry then and still does. I haven't seen her in many years, but I can still remember her and have fond memories of her and her family.

Read Philemon 1:7

As I write this, I should be cleaning my house because I am expecting a visit in a few days from a friend who lives eight hours away. I seldom have the opportunity to visit face to face with her. We don't even talk on the phone or message on social media that often. But she always is a great joy and encouragement to me. Being with her refreshes my heart. We became friends when we worked together. She was actually my boss, but also my friend and mentor. She has become more like family than most of my family. During the time we worked together, both of us experienced some heartbreaking family situations. We both viewed our workplace as a place of ministry, and that was not always easy because of some of our employees and other administrators. We prayed. We cried. And, yes, we laughed. Probably more laughing than crying, because God used our friendship to mutually encourage us in our trust in Him. When God's love works through us, we are encouraged and we also encourage others.

Think of a time when you have been encouraged or have encouraged others because of God's love. Thank Him for those times, and pray that He will continue to use you to encourage others, and that He will provide encouragement for you.

Read 3 John 5-6

HOPE

One of the most encouraging things about God's word is that He shares the accounts of fallible humans who trusted Him. We are able to see that they are sinful. They make mistakes. Let's be honest: they have some pretty heinous sins. Yet God blesses them when they put their trust in Him. The story of David's life is a familiar one. (Read 1 Samuel 16-1 Kings 2 for the biography of David's life.) He was a shepherd boy who God chose as king of Israel after Saul had become arrogant and disobeyed God. When his father sent him to check on his brothers who were involved in the battle with the Philistines, he killed the giant Goliath with a slingshot. He served King Saul as both a valiant soldier and a court musician. Saul became jealous of him because of the successes God gave him in battle. David spent years hiding in the wilderness as Saul attempted time after time to kill him. After he became king, he committed adultery and conspired to commit murder. He made some pretty serious parenting mistakes, resulting in his own son eventually rebelling against him and trying to seize the throne. After his throne was restored, another son tried to take the throne while David was near death. Yet we see that David placed his hope in God, in even the most dire circumstances. A recurring theme in the Psalms is one of placing our hope in God.

Read Psalm 25:3-5

I don't know exactly what was happening in David's life when he wrote this psalm, but we do know that Saul pursued him without cause, with the intent of killing him. David's own son went out to engage his father in battle as David retreated to avoid the conflict. He certainly had experiences where people were treacherous without cause. One of the most difficult situations Christians face is when people who are also believers in Christ treat us treacherously without cause. David's response was to put his hope in God. He prayed that God would show him the right responses and guide his actions. By doing this, he knew that he would not be put to shame. The message is simple. Placing our hope in the Lord gives us strength to face whatever trials we may face.

Read Psalm 33:20-22

We put our hope in the Lord and wait upon Him. We can rejoice in all circumstances when we have wholehearted hope in God, trusting His unfailing love to help us and protect us. When my husband resigned after his accident, the church generously gave us a monetary gift. The way our disability insurance was set up, my husband had to be unable to work full time for 3 months before it would provide benefits. I was able to find a job quickly, but through some sort of administrative error, I did not receive a paycheck for 2 months. Then I experienced an acute health issue that required surgery, causing me to miss 2 ½ weeks of work with no sick leave available. Because of the church's generous gift, we were able to survive for a while, but there came a time when it was increasingly difficult to trust that God would provide. I had even gone through my jewelry box trying to find something to pawn. We kept waiting. Within a day or two of when we would have been unable to pay our bills, we received a check. It was not easy to put our hope in God while we were waiting on Him, but He did not fail us.

Do you find it difficult to put your hope in His unfailing love and wait for His perfect timing? Do you remember times when you waited on the Lord for what seemed like too long, but He answered at just the right time?

Read 1 Peter 3:14-16

The dictionary says that "revere" means to have deep respect for someone. (New Oxford Dictionary) To revere Christ goes much deeper than that. "Revere" is the root word for "reverence". Reverence for God, an understanding and acceptance of Who He Is, enables us to hope unwaveringly. That steadfast hope will be evident to others, even to those who insult you personally and malign the gospel message. People will want to know the reason we have such hope. Because of our understanding of God's character, we will be able to answer their questions.

How would you answer the question, "How can you have such complete hope in this God you serve?"

Peter goes on to tell us that we should answer the question with gentleness and respect. In my opinion, Jerry Falwell was one of the great Christian apologists of our day. He presented a defense of the gospel, explaining to unbelievers the validity of what we believe. He was often seen on secular television talk shows, calmly explaining why He believed the things he believed. He is a wonderful example of what Peter is talking about here. You may want to look up some of his interviews on the news networks and watch.

FRUIT

Paul wrote to the Corinthians, Philippians, and Thessalonians that they should follow his example, just as he followed the example of Christ. We know from many other scriptures that Paul was not prideful nor did he claim to have achieved sinlessness, yet he was confident that God had produced fruit in his life that would serve as an example for others.

Read 1 Corinthians 11:1

Several years ago, a book by Garrett Ward Shelton (Sheldon) started a huge trend with the question, "What Would Jesus Do?" While the commercialization of this phrase was somewhat off-putting to me, the sentiment is the same one Paul tells the Christians in Corinth. Follow the example of Christ. I wish I had the confidence that Paul had– to ask people to follow my example because of my commitment to following Christ's example.

What about you? Do others see fruit in you that reflects Christ? Can you confidently ask others to follow your example of following Christ's example?

Read Philippians 3:16-17

We have all seen the drawings of our uphill climb following Christ's example. We have heard the phrase "one step forward, two steps back", but with our walk with Christ, it is more like "two steps forward, one step back." These illustrations remind us that, in reality, our growth is not a straight arrow toward the target, but there is steady progress toward the goal. Maybe some of us are more like the hare and some are like the tortoise. Paul reminds us to live up to what we have already attained. While we have not attained the ultimate goal, we have made progress. We must not go back.

Make a drawing or share an example showing how you view your growth toward following Christ's example.

One of my younger colleagues at work came into my room and asked if I had any coffee creamer. I had liquid non-dairy creamer, powdered non-dairy creamer, and heavy cream in the refrigerator. She laughed and said, "I want to be just like you when I grow up, always prepared." What if other people looked at our example in following Christ, and said, "I want to be just like you." Wouldn't that be wonderful? I am thankful I had coffee creamer to share with a friend in need, but I want my life to be so much more than coffee creamer. Oh! That others would see Christ in me!

Reflect for a moment on the example others see in you.

Read 2 Thessalonians 3:6-8

As a pastor, my husband has encountered some interesting people, some of them in the church. (see the book of Jude). One man sat in his office discussing some theological questions. The man made the statement, "God put me in the church to be the devil's advocate."

Ponder that a minute.

Paul warns us to stay away from disruptive people, people who are idle, and those who do not follow His (Christ's) example and the teaching they had received.

Read Matthew 7:16-17

The year we moved back to the farm, I planted grape vines, blackberry vines, blueberry bushes, apple trees, peach trees, pear trees, pecan trees, etc. We had an extremely wet spring followed by an extremely dry summer. The plants that didn't drown in the spring dried up and died in the summer. I never saw a single grape, blueberry, blackberry or apple. I can harvest a truck load of weeds though. My attempt at an orchard produced no good fruit at all. Just up the road is a huge orchard which produces all kinds of fruit. Their harvests are shipped all over the country. That orchard produces good fruit. While I was disappointed in the results of my horticulture attempts, that failure is miniscule compared to failure to produce the fruit God expects from us.

Read Galatians 5:21-23

How do we produce the fruit listed in these verses? The Spirit produces them in us. The presence or absence of this fruit is a good indicator of how we are yielding to the Spirit's work in us. Think about the word used here. "Fruit" not "Fruits". When the Spirit dwells in us, He doesn't decide to produce love but not joy, peace but not forbearance...It's a package deal. An all-inclusive package.

One of my husband's friends who was instrumental in bringing my husband to Christ, has a unique way of expressing his beliefs. He said, "I don't judge people, but I'm a fruit examiner."

Examine your own fruit. What do you see?

Read Ephesians 5 1-2, 8-13

This is not something we do, but rather something that comes when we hear the gospel and recognize God's grace. We purposely acknowledge the "who" of God, and our own inability to meet His standards in our own power. A wholehearted devotion to Christ is not so much a "doing" thing, as a "being" thing. The foundation of a wholehearted commitment to Christ is inward, but the results are visible outwardly. So, what are we being? And how is that evident to those around us?

When we are totally committed to Christ, others will see Him in us. Our faith, love, hope, and fruit will be evident. I want to be so much His that others are amazed at how wonderful He is, not even seeing this vessel in which He dwells. I am definitely not where I want to be. My guess would be that you aren't either. But we must not give up. We must commit to an ongoing yielding to Him, allowing Him to produce in us the evidence those around us need to see as a testimony to the whole of who He is.

CHAPTER 3

WHOLEHEARTED RELATIONSHIP

We have discussed the evidence others see in us, but how does that happen? Remember that this is not something we accomplish in our own power or by our own effort. It results from yielding to Him, and a relationship with Him.

- **Colossians 1:9-14 New International Version (NIV) 9 For this reason, since the day we heard about you, we have not stopped praying for you. We continually ask God to fill you with the knowledge of his will through all the wisdom and understanding that the Spirit gives, 10 so that you may live a life worthy of the Lord and please him in every way: bearing fruit in every good work, growing in the knowledge of God, 11 being strengthened with all power according to his glorious might so that you may have great endurance and patience, 12 and giving joyful thanks to the Father, who has qualified you to share in the inheritance of his holy people in the kingdom of light. 13 For he has rescued us from the dominion of darkness and brought us into the kingdom of the Son he loves, 14 in whom we have redemption, the forgiveness of sins.**

RELATIONSHIP WITH GROWTH

BEING FILLED WITH KNOWLEDGE AND WISDOM

Solomon, like his father David, sought God yet failed in many ways to live up to God's standards. Yet God filled him with knowledge and wisdom. (Read 1 Kings 2-11 for the account of Solomon's life.)

Read 1 Kings 4:29

When they were taken into Babylonian captivity, Daniel, Hananiah, Mishael and Azariah remained true to God. God blessed them for their faithfulness and filled them with knowledge and understanding.

Read Daniel 1: 17-20

We sometimes separate the knowledge that God provides from what we would classify as academic knowledge. That is an incorrect assumption. Think about it. God created everything. He is all knowing. He knows every atom of every person, animal, place or thing on this earth. He confounded the languages at Babel (Genesis 11: 1-8) because the people were becoming proud and rejecting Him. (Scripture doesn't specifically use those words.) His purpose in this was not so that He could not understand them, but that they couldn't understand each other. He knows every language spoken on this earth. He can count the stars of the sky. Higher mathematics is not too difficult for Him. He was present when every bit of history, both recorded and that which was not recorded, was made. He is aware of every word written in literature, some which glorify Him and some which break His heart. ALL this knowledge is His, and He is capable of sharing this knowledge with us through His Spirit. When we were homeschooling, we had this one consistent practice. No matter what else we accomplished during the day, we started the day with our Bible lesson, because that was the most important lesson of the day. Admittedly, there were days when it might have appeared that our other classes suffered because of this. When I went back to work, my husband homeschooled for a while, but my son wanted so badly to go to "school" so he could play sports, and because of my husband's health issues, we decided that it was time for public school. Because of their biased opinion of homeschooling, the principal and counselor at the school were apprehensive that my son would not be prepared for the vigorous education he would receive there. However, when he took the standardized testing they required, he scored <u>extremely</u> well. At that point, they were very excited about having him as part of their school.

King Nebuchadnezzar was not interested in the knowledge Daniel, Hananiah, Mishael and Azariah had of the Levitical law, the poetry of David and Solomon, the history of God's plan for the people of Israel. He was not interested in their knowledge of the God he neither acknowledged nor served. He wanted to know things that were academic and even mystical, but definitely not the things we consider scriptural things. But notice that he was astounded with the knowledge and wisdom that God had given to Daniel, Hananiah, Mishael and Azariah.

Read Romans 11:33-34

Read 1 Corinthians 1:4-6

Read Romans 11:33-34 and 1 Corinthians 1: 4-6 again, slowly, pondering the meaning of every word and phrase. In your own words, describe the knowledge of God.

HIS GLORY

Read 2 Corinthians 4:5-7

Write a definition of God's glory.

That was really a trick question. Is it possible to truly define God's glory? We can list some attributes of God. Ezekiel, Isaiah, Daniel, and John all gave us glimpses into the glory of God, but can words truly express the Who of God? Paul reminds the Christians at Corinth that the treasure of God's glory is revealed in our hearts, displayed in the face of Christ, but held in clay jars here on earth. We are those clay jars–opaque vessels. What happens if you try to use a clay pot for a lamp shade? Unlike our electric light bulbs, God's glory is so illuminating that His power shines into and through our clay vessels, revealing His glory. When He, His Glory, dwells in our clay pots, He shines out of our darkness to reach others with His glorious salvation. We can share Him with others. The knowledge of God's glory does not come from us, it shines through us, even in our opaque condition.

MATURITY

Read Ephesians 4:12-14

Paul is reminding the Christians at Ephesus about the purpose of teaching in the church. He lists several components. When we have the knowledge of the Son of God, several other things result.

From this scripture, list some results of growing in the knowledge of the Son of God.

Shallow teaching, false teaching, and lack of commitment on the part of Christians to study and apply God's Word are high on my list of favorite pet peeves. Why do people who have been Christians for decades post things on social media that imply that they believe someone could (or would even want to) leave heaven to visit us in the form of birds, animals or coins? Why do they listen to teachers who take scripture out of context? Why do they get their theology from television, country music, or social media instead of from God's revealed Word? And the list goes on. The answer is both complex and simple. We as Christians don't disciple other Christians in the importance of spiritual growth, growing in the knowledge of God. Our lack of wholehearted devotion to Him results in masses of shallow, baby Christians. As a speech language pathologist, I have worked with children with all sorts of developmental disabilities. Some part of their bodies or minds does not develop as quickly as is considered typical for children their same chronological age. Our churches are full of the spiritually developmentally disabled. The sadness of this is overwhelming. I want to be equipped for works of service, to have unity in the faith, to be mature, to know the whole measure of the fullness of Christ. I don't want to be tossed about by every wind of false doctrine that is so prevalent.

What about you? Will you make a commitment to increase in your knowledge of God, so that you will have the characteristics that Paul lists?

CONTINUING GROWTH

Read 2 Peter 1: 3-9

We don't usually think about the significance of prepositions but look at the word "of" in verses 3 and 8. Notice that it isn't knowledge <u>about</u> Jesus: it is knowledge <u>of</u> Him. This is the difference between head knowledge and heart knowledge. I have some knowledge <u>about</u> some historical figures, political figures, and people in my community. I have knowledge <u>of</u> a much smaller group of people. But knowledge <u>of</u> God is even more personal than the knowledge I have of my closest family members.

Look again at 2 Peter 1: 3-9. Underline what the knowledge of God gives us.

Look at the progression of our growth. Beginning with faith, list the steps in the growth process. Or be creative and draw an illustration of this pattern of growth.

How does this spiritual growth progression protect us?

He calls us to a knowledge of Himself through the salvation He purchased for us on the cross. When we accept that heart knowledge of Him, we receive the promise that we participate in His divine nature through the indwelling of His Spirit within us. We then make the commitment to grow. This growth begins with that faith that led to our salvation and grows in a goodness that comes through yielding to His leadership. This leads to a greater knowledge of Him, which gives us the strength to resist temptation (self-control). From self-control we grow in strength to persevere in whatever temptations and trials we face. Our continued perseverance results in godliness. Godliness is more than just goodness, as in trying to be obedient to God's expectations. Godliness reflects a heart growing more like His heart. When our hearts are more like His, we will have mutual affection for each other. This level of mutual affection indicates that we have true fellowship with other Christians. Then we can love like He loves. His love <u>to</u> us results in His love <u>through</u> us, an unconditional and sacrificial love. This is an ongoing process. We need to have these characteristics in increasing measure. When we do, we are effective and productive in our knowledge of Him. I want to be effective and productive in my knowledge of Him. What about you? To be effective and productive, we must have a commitment to continued spiritual growth.

HIS WILL

Read Mark 3:35

We live in a mobile society. Many jobs require relocation to homes far from family. When people are away from family or in difficult or unusual situations, the people who share their circumstances and location become like family. (See Proverbs 27: 10) I have a friend who is in the Middle East with the petrochemical industry. They often post pictures on social media with friends who are there for the same reason. They are a subculture in a culture very unlike the one to which they are accustomed. My soldier son sees his fellow soldiers as family. And for us who profess Christ as Savior, that family relationship is often within the fellowship of believers. Several years ago, I was fortunate to have two friends who were heart-family. One was the wife of our youth minister. She was a few years younger than me. She was my daughter, niece, my sister, and my friend. The other was a strong Christian work colleague. She was my mother, aunt, my sister, and my friend. Look at how Jesus describes the ones who do God's will. As dear to me as were my two friends, those relationships pale when compared to being called the brother/sister/mother of our Savior. Knowing and doing God's will from a fully committed relationship with Him brings us into an even closer relationship with Him.

Read Romans 12:2

Paul tells the Christians in Rome the way to know God's will. What does he tell them?

At first glance this seems like two distinct steps. But think about it. How do we avoid conforming to the pattern of this world? By renewing our minds. So, the bigger question is: How do we renew our minds? When we are not conformed to this world, and our minds are renewed, then we can discern, test and approve, what is His perfect will.

There are philosophies and false religions running amuck in our world that draw our minds away from the truth we find in God. When our youngest daughter was in kindergarten, we used to call her the New Age Police. When a questionable cartoon came on television, she would run tattling to me that her brothers were watching something New Age. She would bring books home from the school library and promptly bring them to me, informing me that they were New Age. And she was usually correct. Once in a rather futile attempt to support her in her obsession, I took the book she had brought home and asked the librarian to remove the book because it was teaching religion in the school. The librarian said that she could not remove it because the children loved that book. I then told her that children also love books about David and Goliath, Daniel in the Lion's Den, and Joseph's Coat of Many Colors, and that I would love to donate those books to the school library as well. She also refused that request. Looking back, I don't know if I was a good witness to the librarian in trying to address this issue or not. I think that for my daughter's sake, it was the right thing for me to do. As a young innocent child, she understood the importance of keeping our minds from being influenced by things that take the focus off Truth. (I hope that was influenced by what she saw in her parents.) As her mother, I could not squelch that passion in her.

The way to renew our minds is to keep our thoughts focused on the things of God. Our hearts and minds must be wholly committed to His Ways. This is a conscious decision to fill our minds with His Word, to converse with Him in prayer, to let Him work in us and through us to minister to others. Renewing our minds involves growing in our relationship with Him and yielding to Him in every aspect of our lives.

Read 1 Thessalonians 5:12-22

List the things he tells them are God's will for them.

<u>Acknowledge those who work hard among us.</u>
While most people love and appreciate our pastors, teachers and other leaders, we can be offended when the words they speak "step on our toes." We are more likely to acknowledge their hard work when their words encourage us. But when their words convict us and condemn our sin, our human response to those who admonish us (who reprimand us) may be to be angry or upset with them, and not to hold them in the highest regard, as Paul instructs us in 1 Thessalonians 5:13. We might think that they don't understand what is going on in our lives. We have heard the joke, "Pastor, you've stopped preaching and started meddling." So, how is it possible for us to obey the instructions to hold in high regard those who admonish us? When we and our leaders are walking in obedience and commitment to God, we are able to not only understand their motivation, but to appreciate that the words of admonishment are intended to support us in our relationship with God. We allow God to use their teaching, even their reprimands, to bring us closer to Him.

I really like my supervisor at work. I think we have a good relationship and that I can be honest with her. (I explained to her how I felt about this situation, and we did it differently the next year.) At the end of the school year, she had all therapists and special education teachers meet in one place to go through each other's folders and fill out a triplicate form documenting our mistakes. This was very uncomfortable for me. I always try to do my best at my job. If I think that my hard work is appreciated, I will work tirelessly to do my job well. I am open to learning what is expected when it is presented as information that will help me do my job better. However, because I feel that I consistently do the best that I can, I feel defeated if I am publicly criticized for my best efforts. Likewise, I do not want to unduly criticize my co-workers. I prefer to help them if I can. How does this secular workplace situation compare to those who labor among us for Christ? Isn't it better to be supportive and appreciative of God's laborers among us than to criticize them? Can we help them do their job better in some way?

Do you appreciate those who labor among you? How can you be more supportive of their work?

<u>Live in peace with one another.</u>

Generally, people in the churches I have been a part of get along well with each other, and when they occasionally don't, it seems that the cause is really of no consequence at all. A few years ago, I was out of town for our church's business meeting. My husband called me afterwards to tell me how controversial the meeting had been. The wedding committee made recommendations for changes to the wedding policies. Apparently, because our church had a center aisle, people in the community who did not hold our views on marriage wanted to rent the church for their weddings. The committee's recommendations were to specify what requirements should be met for the church to allow couples to use the church auditorium. On the surface, it seemed a reasonable response that would allow others to be married at our facilities without compromising our beliefs. For some reason, some of the others in the church took these recommendations as personal insults. The discussion was heated. Before it got completely out of hand, my husband called for a motion for the recommendations to be tabled and the meeting adjourned. As comical as this seems in retrospect, it speaks to a serious matter. We need to live in peace with each other. Why do we argue? Are we self-serving or self-sacrificing? My husband loves movies, mostly older ones, but also some of the newer ones. He often quotes movies, but I have no idea what he is talking about. I had heard this quote from "Mars Attack" many times, but had to look it up to share it here. "Why can't we all just get along?" (Burton) Sometimes we may feel like our fellow Christians are from other planets; they are not and are just as much a part of the family of God as are we. As Christians we should not be like the Martians and Earthlings in this movie. We should get along with each other in a spirit of love and respect. That doesn't mean we won't have disagreements, but we live peacefully with each other.

Have you ever participated in an unnecessary controversy or argument with your Christian brothers and sisters? What could have been done differently so that you could live in peace with each other?

Warn those who are idle and disruptive.

Anyone who has worked with children, or who is a parent, understands how these two words go together. What happens when a child has nothing to do? When our older children were small, we used church bulletins and pencils, fingerplays, head rubs, etc. to keep them occupied during church so they wouldn't be disruptive. Any teacher who doesn't give the children a task to do while she tries to work with another child will end up dealing with a disruptive child. A Christian who is not actively involved in serving God will become disruptive. My daddy often quoted his grandmother "Idle hands are the devil's workshop." There is truth in that statement. Is idleness a choice or a circumstance? I think it is a choice. A person may choose not to minister to others. I have heard that 20% of the people in a church do 80% of the work. Why is that? Because they are bossy and overbearing? I don't think so. They do things because no one else is willing to minister. So, what are those other 80% of the people doing? Very little. Are they being disruptive? Possibly. I will stretch this point to include gossip under the umbrella of disruption. We all have known people who are "in everyone's business." Even one who is homebound chooses to either participate in some productive activity or to participate in some unproductive activity. The word "warn" has strong connotations. We know the difference between a weather watch and a weather warning. Warnings are serious and require us to take action. My daughter-in-law and I keep each other informed of weather events. We text "Are you watching the weather?" because we are concerned about each other. We will warn the idle person, not because we condemn them, but because we are concerned about them. The warning comes from a heart of love for our brothers and sisters. How do we warn the idle person? The meteorologist warns us of impending weather events by providing factual documentation that supports and explains the reason for the warning. Scripture is how we warn others. My words of warning have very little effect if they are not supported by God's Word.

Do we love our brothers and sisters enough to warn them about their idleness? Or are we sitting by while they disrupt the ministry God has for His local church? What should you do differently than you are doing now?

Are you being idle and disruptive? Repent now and commit to a life of purposeful ministry.

Encourage the disheartened.

Have you ever felt disheartened? I have. We all need encouragement sometimes. Sometimes we are discouraged by simple things. There is way too much laundry or the house isn't clean enough to suit us. Other times discouragement comes from significant setbacks in our lives. Job loss, rebellious children, illness, deaths, and the list goes on. Sadly, however, often those periods of discouragement come from things that happen within the church body. From my own experience, encouragement from others often brings the pain to the surface. We may be holding it together, barely, but when someone sees our need and reaches out, we fall apart. I've had that happen more than once, and

I imagine you have too. We need to be aware of the discouragement of others and be willing to encourage them. Sometimes, that may just be a hug and a box of tissues. Other times that may be an act of service. Be open to what God leads you to do.

Think about ways that you can encourage someone today. Do you need encouragement? As hard as it may be, let someone know that.

<u>Help the weak.</u>

I like to think that I am strong. My aunt once told me "You came from pioneer stock," which is true. As I have shared with you, my great-great grandfather homesteaded the land where we now live. But family history is not where we grow truly strong. Our strength comes from God, and we are obligated to use that strength for His glory. I tend to be willing to help those who are weak because of their backgrounds, and lack of exposure to the Truth. When I made home visits to work with children between birth and three years old who had developmental disabilities, I also helped the parents learn how to work with their children. Some of these homes were not clean and the people were not what I would call outstanding parents, to say the least. One parent met me at the door, told me she had to go somewhere, and just left. That was the first time I ever went to their home. I wasn't even sure she would come back. The living room floor had a hole in it large enough for a child to fall through. There were roaches and trash everywhere. I carried my materials in a plastic container and sat on that container rather than on the floor or in a chair, for fear of the bugs that would crawl on me. I have repented that more than once I prayed that they would not be home when I went for the home visits there. One day, in the course of the conversation, the mother asked me about a certain skill (cutting with scissors) she wanted her daughter to have. I explained that she had to develop other skills before that particular skill could be developed. As an illustration, I explained that I made my children a checklist for cleaning their rooms: I could not just tell them to clean. They needed specific details. The mother asked me if I could bring her a copy of that list. I did so. The next time I went to her house, it was clean. No one had ever told her what she needed to do to clean the house! I won't go into details about the "man" who lived there, but I have jokingly said that his picture is beside the dictionary definition for "surly and irresponsible" (I may have used a slang term instead) and I overheard him (from the bed at 11:00 a.m.) refer to me as "that loudmouth". After over a year of home visits, she informed me that they were moving to a different state, then she said, "You are the best friend I have had here." Wow! I was paid to go to her home to work with her child, and she saw me as her best friend! This whole experience opened my eyes to how circumstances and a cycle of lifestyles affect people. This woman wanted better, but she didn't know how. That is true weakness. She, and others like her, need help. The downside to that is that I may not be particularly sympathetic to those I perceive as weak, when that happens to be someone who is in a leadership position in the church who should have developed some maturity. That has caused me some trouble, as you can imagine. Enough said. So, I have learned some difficult lessons. It is not my place to condemn someone who is weak. It is my responsibility to help them. Even in the events following my husband's wreck, we have dealt with this issue. Because of his health, I have had added responsibilities to help him. I'm not saying he is weak, but he has needed me to step up to the plate and do some things that he has done in the past. This has been very difficult for him. Honestly, there are some parts of these lessons that I have not completely figured out. But God doesn't ask us to understand. He asks us to obey Him. He commands us to help the weak. The attitude of our hearts must be one of love, not condemnation. We don't help because we are stronger or better in any way. We help because God calls us to do so.

Pray about this. How do you help the weak without insulting them or hurting their feelings by the implication that we are stronger?

Be patient with everyone.

I have a student who has a long history of being distractible, disobedient, and not doing well academically. He has been in trouble as long as I have known him. He has had some excellent teachers who have patiently worked with him, but to be honest, he has tried the patience of every teacher he has ever had. As his speech language pathologist, I have told him more times than I can count to sit in his chair correctly and to attend to tasks. A few months ago, I had the opportunity to start working with him individually instead of in a group. With just that little extra time, he has shown so much improvement. He is excited to be learning, and works harder than I ever imagined that he would. He has taught me a lesson in patience. While I often dreaded the constant reminders to attend to tasks and was concerned about his lack of progress, the persistent patience of several people and some extra time has changed him. Think about how patient God is with us. There are probably times He sees me in the same way I saw this child. Yet He is persistently patient with me. We are to treat others in the same way.

Are there people with whom you need to be more patient? Are there situations where you need to exercise more patience? Pray for God's strength in these situations.

Don't pay back wrong for wrong.

This seems straightforward. But, have you ever stewed over the hurt someone has caused you, thought about all the things you wish you had said, or formulated a plan to hurt them in the same way. Of course, we never really intend to do those things but the attitude of our hearts is revengeful. Paying back wrong for wrong is as much about our attitude as our actions.

Pray that God will give you an attitude that does not desire retribution for wrongs done toward you.

<u>Strive to do what is good for each other.</u>
New Orleans, particularly the Ninth Ward, was devastated by Hurricane Katrina. Evacuees flooded (no pun intended) into southeast Texas via Interstate 10. Golden Triangle Baptist Association had recently acquired an old nursing home facility for the purpose of providing lodging to families who came to visit their loved ones in the federal prisons in the area. The association opened this facility to the evacuees. The facilities were quickly filled to capacity. They asked churches in the area to provide additional living areas. By God's grace we had a home at the time that had a "guest house". The family who came to live in that guest house had lost nearly everything when nine feet of water covered their home. We were able to do something good for them by allowing them to stay with us. However, the greatest good we could do for them was to share the gospel with them. Sadly, they did not accept Christ as their Savior while they were living with us. This scripture tells us to "strive" to do what is good. "Strive" means to make a great effort, but does not guarantee success. While this family didn't accept Christ while they were with us, a seed was planted, and we strove to do what was good for them.

Are you striving to do what is good for others?

<u>Rejoice always.</u>
A sweet friend was dying of cancer. She made a list of things she liked about having cancer. Among other things she mentioned that her friends came to see her, and that she could eat whatever she wanted without gaining weight. She was looking on the bright side and seeking to rejoice in the face of cancer and impending death. I'm trying to remember if I have rejoiced when difficult circumstances have come my way. Sadly, I cannot say that I have. But scripture tells us to rejoice always.

Pray that God will help you to rejoice always, not just when circumstances are good.

<u>Pray continually.</u>
When we define prayer as closing our eyes and talking to God, this scripture is difficult to implement. However, our hearts should be constantly open for communication with God. In close personal relationships, we don't talk all the time. And when we do talk, it isn't one person who does all the talking. But when we are together, we are responsive to communication from the other person. (Unless of course one of you is watching television, right?) In much the same way, we are continually with God and ready to communicate with Him and He with us.

<u>Give thanks in all circumstances.</u>
Our thankfulness is not dependent on circumstances. We are thankful based on our relationship with God. Many times, our lives are like the Hee-Haw (Frank Peppiatt) skit where a bad situation results in a good situation and visa-versa.

Let's write a little skit of our own. "My husband was in a car wreck caused by a drunk driver–That's bad–No-that's good. They did a complete examination when he was taken to the emergency room–That's good–No, that's bad. When he was being triaged from the accident, they found kidney cancer–That's bad-No, that's good. If he hadn't had the wreck, they wouldn't have found the cancer early-That's good." etc. The point is that God works everything out perfectly according to His plan. We aren't thankful for individual events as much as we are thankful that He works all things together. We give thanks in all things.

<u>Don't quench the spirit.</u>
The word "quench" in this context means to extinguish the fire, or to stifle or suppress. The Spirit of God works in us. We should allow Him complete control in our lives. We had an older relative living with us for a while. She believes that God randomly chooses those He wants to save, and that people have no choice, no freewill. God had been speaking to me for a long time to talk to her about accepting Him as her Savior. The Spirit was gently telling me I should talk to her but I resisted because she has a quick temper and a tendency to harbor bitterness. I didn't want to be the recipient of her anger. One Sunday morning, God really started convicting me. It is hard to explain, but it was like a physical pressure on me, a feeling that it was now or never. I began to think that she might die that day without Christ if I didn't say something to her right then. Truthfully, it was frightening. I have never felt His guidance so urgently. I won't repeat the entire conversation, but I asked her if she knew for sure that she would go to heaven when she died. I explained the plan of salvation to her. My fears of her reaction were entirely justified. She was furious, screaming at me that I should know that she is a good person. It was terrible, yet it was wonderful, because I had such complete assurance that I had acted in obedience to God's work in my life, even if it wasn't what I wanted to do, and didn't get the results I would have liked to have seen. Our own will or our personal fears should never take precedence over His work in and through us. This is the essence of living a wholehearted life for God.

Do you remember any time that God's Spirit was prompting you to take action, or to wait, and that you quenched His Spirit in you by following your own desires.

Can you think of times that you have complete confidence that you did not quelch the work of the Spirit in your life?

<u>Don't treat prophecies with contempt but test them all.</u>
We should listen to the preaching and teaching of God's Word, but we have the personal responsibility of making sure that what is being taught is true to scripture. I am telling this story because it is comical in a way, but also deeply saddening when the implications are considered. I was asked to be assistant teacher in a senior adult ladies' Sunday School class. The ladies were a tight

knit group who loved to visit and keep up with their prayer gossip list. (You know what I mean by that.) Very little actual Bible study was taking place, and even that study was not always scriptural. One Sunday I was deeply disturbed by at least four statements that were clearly not consistent with scripture. I prayed all week about how God would lead me to address this. On Saturday I compiled a list of scriptures addressing those four statements, made copies and handed them to the class members Sunday morning. I said something like "The discussion last week gave me some food for thought so I looked some things up in the Bible and thought I would share with you what I found in scripture about what was discussed." The teacher quit. All but one of the ladies was suddenly in too poor health to come to Sunday School, but frequently made it for church. At the end of the Sunday School year, the former teacher asked for her class back. Miraculously, all the ladies' health immediately improved and they came back to Sunday School. They did not want to hear scriptural teaching. They enjoyed the social situation but were not interested in correct theology. Don't misunderstand. I am not angry with them nor are my feelings hurt. I actually think it's funny in a way, but I am sad that they are missing out on what scripture has to teach them. I do not regret standing up for scriptural integrity. I do not think I was rude or confrontational. This is one instance where I feel like I did the right thing.

Hold onto what is good.

In Matthew 19: 17, Jesus tells the rich ruler that there is only one who is good. When we hold on to what (who) is good, we are holding onto God. The context here refers to the teaching of God as revealed through scripture. We must be vigilant to recognize the misrepresentation of God through false teaching. Television and the paid programming of televangelists has long been a source of false teaching mixed with those who truly preach and teach God's word. What I believe is even more dangerous and more prevalent is social media. I never cease to be amazed at the falsehood posted as truth by people who profess to be Christians. We must be students of the scriptures so that we will recognize what is false and separate truth from heresy. We must hold onto what is good and reject what is false.

Reject every kind of evil

Rejecting evil in the world around us is a monumental task. We cannot do it unless we allow God's Spirit to work in us. A wholehearted commitment to Him is the only way to reject every kind of evil. I cannot write to you that I am successful in rejecting every kind of evil. I am certain that you cannot honestly say that you do either. We input evil through television and the internet, and those things are not necessarily things that would be considered overtly evil. Evil is subtle and not easily recognizable without the Spirit's guidance in our lives. We also have evil within us that comes from our attitudes and desires. We are exposed to evil in our workplaces, and even in our own homes. We must be constantly yielded to Him and vigilant in our avoidance of evil.

Are you avoiding evil or have you allowed evil to creep into your life?

Read 1 Peter 2:15-16

A few employees were obviously inebriated at a charity event sponsored by the children's rehabilitation center where I worked. There were some interactions between married (not to each other) and single persons that would not be considered appropriate, at least by my standards. Since I was the therapy director at the time, some, but not all, of these people were under my supervision at work, but not necessarily so at a charity event. (I have been known to make some uncalculated decisions regarding standing up for my convictions.) I contacted the CEO of the program, who was ultimately responsible for what happened at this event. I explained to her that I was concerned that we were not presenting an image in the community that reflected our commitment to providing a wholesome environment for the children. I did not mention names, but spoke in generalities about the actions I observed. The events that followed were stressful for me, because I loved my job, and knew that God had sent me there. But, ultimately, because of my work record, my relationships with others in the facility, and God's grace and work in my life, their ignorant talk was silenced. In fact, it wasn't long before I was promoted to assistant administrator. I am certainly not saying that my life and example were what I would have desired them to be, but in seeking to serve God through my work, He protected me from those who sought to do me harm. One of these people became a friend that I can network with in professional matters. Out of, or in spite of this situation, we developed a good relationship.

Can you think of a time when God silenced the ignorant talk of foolish people because of your commitment to do His will? Share that here.

Read 1 Peter 4:1

A friend suffered from cancer and was taking chemotherapy treatments. These treatments were provided to several patients at a time. They were all in one room and sat there together for quite a while. My friend began singing hymns and songs of praise. Others began to join her. This became their consistent practice, a chemotherapy choir who sang every time they were together. While they were suffering, they turned that suffering into praise and worship.

Share an example, either in your own life or of someone you observed, who continued to do good even when they were suffering according to God's will.

Why do you think these people were able to continue to do good in the midst of suffering?

CHAPTER 4

RESULTS OF RELATIONSHIP

WISDOM

Read Psalm 111:9-10

I'm not sure why, but when I think of a wise person, I envision an old man with a long gray beard, wearing a flowing muslin robe and sitting cross-legged on a beautiful mountain top. But that isn't correct. Wisdom has nothing to do with age, appearance, apparel, or location. Wisdom comes from reverence of who God is. Verse 9 says that His name is holy and awesome. When scripture mentions the name of God, it is not simply a few letters strung together to help identify a person. The name of God means the whole of who He is, every characteristic of the undefinable God. Wisdom begins when we recognize, accept, and reverence the Name of God. (See Proverbs 8)

Take a moment to consider the Name of God. Praise Him through prayer now with reverent fear.

Read Proverbs 2: 1-6

In many professions there are "If...then" concepts and statements. An example in my profession would be "Given instruction, example, and activity, (child) will produce voiceless /th/ in the initial position of words with 90% accuracy by the end of the school year." Yours might be quite different. Perhaps it would be that if you invest in this project, you would expect a certain profit or result. Even children have these if/then statements. "If you clean your room, then we will go to the park."

Think about the "if/then" concepts in your daily life. Look at this passage from Proverbs 2: 1-6, and write an "If...then" statement about gaining wisdom and understanding. You may want to write a list instead of just one statement.

Read Luke 21:14-16

I have never had to defend myself against adversaries like the early disciples did, but I have facilitated some Bible studies. In that context I have heard statements which were so shockingly inaccurate that they needed to be addressed immediately, but were something that I had not anticipated nor had I prepared a response. At those times I sensed a total dependence on God giving me the right words to say.

I have also faced situations and had conversations with my children that I could not address without God giving me the words to say. I cannot say that I have faced every situation that you may have faced, but as a family, we have experienced many heartbreaks and trials. Have I always listened to God and allowed Him to give me the words to say? Honestly, no. But I know that the times I have listened, His words have been the right thing to say.

Have there been times when you felt a total dependence on God to give you the words to say?

Read Acts 6:5-11

Notice the description of Stephen in verse 5. He was full of faith and of the Holy Spirit. Verse 8 tells us that Stephen was full of God's grace and power. Then verse 10 tells us that those who opposed could not stand up against the wisdom that the Spirit gave Stephen. This opposition that arose was not against Stephen specifically, but was against the word of God, the gospel that was spreading in Jerusalem. Think about how all this is intertwined. Stephen was full of faith and of the Holy Spirit, which resulted in grace, power, and wisdom in the face of opposition against the spread of the gospel. We cannot expect God to give us wisdom unless we are fully committed to Him. Even then, the purpose of the wisdom He gives us is for the advancement of the gospel and for His glory, not our own personal gain or even safety. As we finish the reading of Acts 6, we know that Stephen was martyred by stoning after speaking with such wisdom that the opposition could not stand up against him.

Read 1 Corinthians 1: 22-31

You have likely encountered, as have I, those I would label as educational or intellectual snobs. In their opinion, their intelligence, level of education, or educational institution is vastly superior to anyone else's. Paul makes it clear that our boasting cannot be in our own intelligence or education. I have also witnessed the trend in academia to belittle the wisdom of God, treating His Word as myth and superstition. This goes beyond snobbery, which is slightly annoying to us of lesser intelligence and education, and becomes a mockery of God, the most heartbreaking of conditions. I have family members in this state. My heart aches for them, as I pray for their salvation. You probably know someone like this as well. Take a moment now to pray for their salvation.

My husband has a Doctor of Ministry from a well-recognized seminary, but when anyone calls him "Doctor Webb", he tells them, "I'm Brother Bryan. A doctorate is like putting a tail on a pig. It doesn't change the flavor of the bacon."

The dictionary definition of wisdom (New Oxford Dictionary) has to do with experience, knowledge, and good judgment. Paul defines God's wisdom differently in 1 Corinthians 1:30. God's wisdom is our righteousness, holiness and redemption. God's wisdom has to do with our salvation and commitment to Him, which produces righteousness and holiness, not of our own power but the result of God's Spirit at work in us. God's wisdom is greatly superior to the world's definition of wisdom.

Look back through the ways Paul lists that God's wisdom is superior. List or describe those.

Read 1 Corinthians 2: 1-16

I do not know the origin of this quote but have heard it used as an illustration often. "My pastor is so smart: I don't understand a word he says." Paul was an educated man, probably one of the most educated within the Jewish community at that time. Yet, he resolved to know nothing but Christ crucified. He did not flaunt his worldly wisdom, but focused on the wisdom of God. That same wisdom is available to all who will trust Him wholeheartedly. When the Spirit of God indwells us, we have the mind of Christ. Mull that over for a minute. That is an extremely powerful statement.

Read 1 Corinthians 2: 1-16 again. Compare the wisdom of God and the wisdom of the world.

Explain how we are able to understand the things of God.

In other scriptures Paul reminds us that he had not obtained the level of maturity which he desired, but in this particular scripture, he encourages us with the thought that we are able to grow spiritually. Spiritual growth is dependent on the Spirit revealing the mind of Christ to us. His wisdom is given freely to those who love Him. Spiritual growth is not dependent on educational level, social class, or intelligence.

Read Ephesians 1:7-9

All scripture is God's Word and deserves our full attention. I would never say otherwise. But it seems to me that some scripture begs to be contemplated with awe and amazement. (Truthfully, all scripture has that same significance.) Right now, think about this particular passage (Ephesians 1: 7-9) and consider its significance for you on a personal level. Think for a moment about every word and short phrase. Every word in these verses speaks to me powerfully. Redemption. Forgiveness. Riches of God's grace. Lavished! Lavished on us! All wisdom. All understanding. The mystery of His will. His good pleasure. Purposed in Christ. Wow!

After prayerfully contemplating Ephesians 1: 7-9 summarize how these three verses interconnect.

God's purpose in Christ was that we would be redeemed and forgiven of our sin according to the riches of His grace. Think about how rich God is in grace. Then He lavished this on us. I can't get this word out of my head. Lavished! And His purpose was to give us all wisdom and understanding so that we can know the mystery of His will.

Now, let's think about prepositions again. "In Him." To receive this lavish grace, we must be IN HIM. Have you ever been in a situation or watched a movie where the question was asked, "Are you in or are you out?" The implication was "Are you fully committed to this endeavor?" To be in Christ means a fully committed, wholehearted relationship with Him. Then, He lavishes all these blessings on us.

Are you receiving his <u>lavish</u> grace? "Are you in or are you out?" in your relationship with Christ.

Read Ephesians 1:16-18

This prayer that Paul prayed for the Christians at Ephesus is my prayer for myself and for you. Again, stop a few minutes and contemplate the things Paul desires for his fellow believers.

Read James 1:4-6

(Strange how many times as I write that I need to preface an illustration with "right now I…") Right now, I have an extreme lack of wisdom to deal with a certain situation. I am praying for wisdom, but truthfully, I am struggling with doubt that a good end will come to it. We have a family member who is old enough to be called an adult, but has shown no signs of maturity on any level. For over a year, he has been making very bad decisions. At first, I was angry and frustrated, but the last episode has left me only disappointed, sad, and with a sense of helplessness and hopelessness. It's difficult to let perseverance finish its work in some situations. I am also dealing with the fear that the wisest decision may be something that will crush my heart. I am struck with the realization that God's wisdom is infinitely greater than anything that we can comprehend, and that when we ask for His wisdom, without wavering, He may reveal a path that is painful, but will result in something wonderful that we may not even understand. Maybe you have been in a similar situation, one where you were hopeless and helpless without God revealing His wisdom to you. If you are in the midst of this struggle, it may be very painful to share. If God has brought you through with victory, you have a great testimony that will encourage others.

What situation are you experiencing, or have you experienced, that is teaching or has taught you about perseverance through adversity, trusting God, and depending on His wisdom without doubt?

SPIRITUAL UNDERSTANDING

Read Psalm 49: 3

The dictionary defines meditation as "thinking deeply or carefully about something." (New Oxford Dictionary) Even when we make the effort to have a quiet time every day, do we really think deeply and carefully about what His word says, or do we read hurriedly and go on about our lives? I am as guilty as anyone about this. Get up at 5:00 a.m., read for 30 minutes (including checking the weather for the day, updates on social media and any national or local news that I find interesting.) Then hop in the shower, dress, make my "to go" cup of coffee and head out the door to work. How can we have understanding unless we meditate on what God's word teaches us? This goes again to the point that a wholehearted commitment to God is not about commitment to a routine or ritual. It is about true relationship.

All of Psalm 119 speaks of gaining understanding. Take a few minutes to read the entire chapter from your Bible or Bible app. Underline or list ways God speaks to you about His wisdom.

Let's look briefly then at verses 32-35.

Reread Psalm 119: 32-35

We start our walk, our commitment to God, based on an understanding based on faith. God broadens and deepens our understanding, thus giving us the strength to "run" in that path. The wonderful and frustrating thing about our English language is that words can have so many different meanings. "Run" can mean simply putting one foot in front of the other with bended knees, but the meaning here is much richer. I envision a large factory, with each worker and each machine doing exactly what should be done, producing amazing finished products. The factory is running at full production. Now apply that concept to what happens when we run in the path of God's commands.

I recently attended my uncle's funeral. The pastor talked about remaining faithful to the end. We sometimes talk about the "used to be" people. They used to be there every Sunday. They used to be in the choir. They used to be a Sunday School teacher. They used to be…Why are there so many "used to be" church members? Because they did not accept the broadened understanding that God is willing to give, and they did not follow to the end. Harsh words, maybe, but we have to be honest. God's understanding allows us to obey with all our hearts. When He directs us in the path of His commands, we are delighted to follow them. There are earthly things that give me delight. I delight in french fries, homemade yeast rolls, lemon icebox pie, cherry cheesecake… When my doctor told me that a low carb lifestyle would be healthier for me, it was very difficult to give up those things that were delightful for me. If we find delight in following God's paths, it is not easy to give up the time we spend with Him or the ministry He calls us to do.

Are there things that are more delightful to you than following God's path? Confess that as sin, repent, and ask God to help you develop priorities for Him.

Read 1 John 5:19-20

Because Jesus came, we can have understanding and know God. We not only know God, but we are in Him because of Jesus' sacrifice for us. Think about how important the preposition "in" is. It can be hot outside, and I can be <u>by</u> the pool but it does not help me cool off until I am <u>in</u> the pool. I can be <u>near</u> the storm shelter when a tornado is coming directly toward me, but it doesn't save my life unless I am <u>in</u> the storm shelter. And we have seen the social media descriptions of a person as "in a relationship." Putting those last two illustrations together in a strange way. (I hope you understand my sense of humor.) I am in a marriage relationship with my husband, but he is the one who would be standing outside the storm shelter, watching the tornado. I am the one who insists that he come inside the shelter. When we are in a relationship with Jesus, He makes sure we are sheltered from the storms. The storms will still come, but when we accept the understanding that Jesus gives to us and are in Him, we are safe. Another common phrase "…someone who <u>is in the know</u>…" implies a person is in a close enough relationship with the parties making major decisions to know what is about to happen or what has already happened, and to understand the implications. Because of Jesus, we can be "in the know" about God.

Think about your relationship with Christ. Are you "in the know" or standing outside looking in?

I admit that I like country music. I sometimes even gather spiritual truths that were not intended by the songwriter. (For instance, for a long time I thought the song "Dust on the Bottle" (Murphy) was "Dust on the Bible". The principle applies.) There is also a song, "Standing Outside the Fire" (Brooks) which doesn't really mean something scriptural, but again, the concept applies. I know that it's a stretch, but (if you are willing to) listen to this song and apply the concept of being <u>in</u> the fire of a relationship with God. We know that Moses saw God in the burning bush, Elijah was taken up into heaven in a chariot of fire, and that the Holy Spirit appeared as tongues of fire on the Day of Pentecost. Our life is merely survived, not truly lived, if we stand outside the Fire.

WALKING WORTHY

Read Matthew 10:37-38

Priorities: Obviously, it is not wrong to love our parents or our children. So, what is Jesus saying here? If we love anyone more than Him, we are not worthy. In different stages of our lives, we have the temptation to make family our priority, rather than to let Jesus have priority. There are young adults who resist leaving the safety of their parent's community to follow God's leadership. There are young parents who place their children before God. And the list goes on. This temptation affects every age group from the time a child reaches the realization of his or her need for Christ until we worship Him in Heaven.

I love my grandchildren. Four of them live closer than the others, so I get to spend more time with them. They will periodically spend the night here. One of them is a very early riser. I'm not sure it is even possible to set your alarm to get up early enough to spend time with God before she wakes up. And she wakes up happy and perky and talkative. Luckily, I'm a morning person too, but not as much as she is. Over the years we have established a routine. She knows that I read my Bible first thing in the morning. She will get her Bible and read too. I can't say that she can read quietly just yet, but she is young. She is learning that I love her, but that God has priority. (She is actually the first one in our family that this has been an issue. There are no other morning people in our family, just this sweet girl and her nanna.) Our families need to understand that we love them completely, but that God is more important to us, and that He should also be more important to them than we are.

I don't know where you are in your life stage right now, but take a moment to reflect. Do you have a stronger love for your earthly family than you do for God?

If we hold any human in higher priority, or with greater love than we do Jesus, we are not worthy of Him. If we are to walk worthy, we have to establish in our hearts the total commitment of our love for Him.

Read Acts 5:40-42

The apostles were flogged. Flogging would have been 39 lashes. I can only imagine how painful and humiliating that would be. Think about adults being paddled relentlessly in a public forum.

Granted, cultures are different now, but I can't help comparing how that would feel, emotionally and physically, based on our present standards. While floggings were a common punishment in that era, the shame and pain would not have been much different. Yet they rejoiced that they were considered worthy of suffering disgrace, and continued teaching and evangelizing. Walking worthy is not always pleasant. Thankfully, we are not flogged for proclaiming the gospel. But there are hardships, even in our times. Notice that the apostles continued to teach and proclaim the good news that Jesus is the Messiah. They did not let their circumstances change their commitment.

The important part is being consistent in our commitment, even in the face of unpleasant circumstances. Are you consistent in your walk or do your circumstances affect your commitment to God?

Read Ephesians 4:1-3

This is another one of those scriptures that I have to ponder and allow the Spirit to speak to me. Such conviction! Living a life worthy of our calling means applying these things to all areas of our lives. It is much easier for me to be gentle, patient and bear with people outside my family. For several years I have had a struggle to apply this to a certain situation in my family. It is too private and sensitive to explain here, so suffice it to say that I struggle with this daily. Very often I am not walking worthy of the calling I have received. (I promised you I would be honest.) I pray about it. I ask for strength. I try really hard to maintain the bond of peace. I find myself to be trapped between two emotions, anger or sobbing tears of grief for what should have been. Most of the time, I internalize it because I don't want to hurt the other family member, but sometimes I just can't keep it all to myself. That is when the bond of peace is broken with others. My point is that walking worthy is not easy, even when we really want to do so.

I know you are probably thinking that I am a hypocrite for even trying to write this Bible study, after what I just shared with you. And you are absolutely correct. I want to make it clear that I fail terribly, and as I stated earlier, the study is more for myself than for you.

Do some self-searching here. Are you walking worthy of the calling you received, even in those private, family situations that the rest of the world, even your church family, doesn't see. Pray for God's strength that whatever situation is most difficult for you.

Read Philippians 1:27-28

What do these verses tell us will be the evidence that we are conducting ourselves in a manner worthy of the gospel? What will be the result?

I am struck by the first two words in this passage. "Whatever happens." Think about all the "whatever happenings" in your life, those instances where life throws you a curve that you weren't expecting, or where what happened was not what your desired outcome would have been. Then skip down to verse 28, "This is a sign to them…" Our responses to the "whatever happenings" will be a testimony to the lost of their lostness. When we stand firm in our faith, work together as the body of Christ, and are unafraid of opposition, they will see the power of Christ in our lives. While our relationship with Christ is a very personal, intimate one, the outcome of that relationship is visible to those around us. Walking worthy of the calling is not something done in a vacuum and can have a convicting effect on those around us. Conversely, and this is the terrifying part, when we do not walk worthy of the calling, others see that too, and there are consequences for others of our unworthy walk.

Read 1 Thessalonians 2:11-13

The Christians at Thessalonica had accepted Paul's teaching of the word of God as a message sent from God, not simply something Paul had invented. Because they received in faith, God's word was at work in their lives. Paul encouraged them to live lives worthy of God. This worthy walk is only possible because of the work of God in the lives of those who believe. We have heard "Don't get the cart before the horse." This principle applies here. We cannot live worthy lives unless God's word is at work in us. There are theological points that Jesus is the "logos", the Word of God. There is also the word of God, which refers to the written revelation of God in scripture. Both of these concepts are pertinent here. Unless we have the Spirit of Christ indwelling us, and unless we are familiar with the scripture through reading and study, we cannot live worthy lives. As we read the scripture, His Spirit works in us to guide us in the way we should live.

How do you view God's Word, both the written word and Jesus, the Word? Are you studying the written word? Are you allowing the Word to work in you?

Read 2 Thessalonians 1:10-12

The purposes of our walking worthy of God's calling are that the name of Jesus be glorified in us, which I understand to be a testimony to those around us, and for us to be glorified in Him, which I understand to be not earthly glorification, but heavenly glory. This is accomplished through His power when we desire to walk worthy, when our actions are prompted by faith, and when our faith is supported by our actions. We desire it, then God does it. The key is to strongly desire to walk worthily by faith, and allow Him to bring it to fruition. Then, and only then, is He glorified in us.

What is your heart's desire?

CHAPTER 5

RESULTS OF RELATIONSHIP-PART 2

FULLY PLEASING TO HIM

Read Psalm 19:13-14

Reread Psalm 19: 13-14 as a heartfelt prayer.

I want everything that I say, and everything that I think about to be pleasing in God's sight. I don't want to purposely sin. I don't want my own sinfulness to control my life. I want to be blameless. I'm sure you want the same things too. But, let's be honest. How well are you doing at this? Me neither. Read the first part of verse 13 again. We do not keep ourselves from willful sins; God does that when we yield to Him.

There is quite a lot of paperwork in my job. We "hold folders" on our students. Those folders are monitored every three years by the Department of Education. They have to be done correctly or we are in trouble. Sometimes, I have to share folders with someone else, if that child receives services other than speech therapy. I hate that. I want to do everything by myself. I don't trust anyone else to do things as well as I want them to, and I don't want to be held accountable for someone else's mistakes. (Pride and controlling tendencies confessed.) I don't mind being held accountable for my own mistakes, and I most certainly make them. I own those. But I don't own someone else's mistakes. Think about this. Don't you think God can do much better with our "folders" than we can! He never makes mistakes. Yet, he sacrificed Himself on the cross so that He could own our sins for us. He paid the price for our sin. We need to let Him work in our lives, protect us, guide us, teach us. Only through Him can we be free of willful sin and blameless.

Last Sunday in our Sunday School class, a young man who had been raised in church told us that he had "made a profession of faith" as a child because that is what all his friends were doing, but that as a young adult, he realized that he needed to be saved. For him, it was a relief because he had been trying in his own effort to do all the right things. When he let God be the one who kept him from willful sin, his life was much less stressful. Allowing God to protect us is so much easier than trying to do everything by ourselves.

Read Romans 12:1-3

Offering ourselves as living sacrifices is a pretty clear way of stating that we have wholehearted commitment to Him.

Why do we offer our bodies as living sacrifices?

We offer our bodies as living sacrifices because of God's mercy. God's mercy is only of significance to us when we realize that we deserve His judgment. There is no need for mercy without the recognition of transgression. We offer ourselves as living sacrifices because we understand our own sinfulness, have accepted Christ's sacrificial gift of salvation, and respond in grateful wholehearted submission and dependence on His mercy.

How are we made pleasing to God?

We please God by the renewing of our minds. The only way to avoid conforming to the world is to allow God to transform and continually renew our minds. I'm looking at the top of my computer screen to that little partial circle with an arrow. It lets me refresh my connection to a particular site. I have to make an effort to do that. But I also see a notification at the top center of my screen which says "saving". I like using this program for my documents because it constantly saves all my work. I remember those times when I forgot to save something I was working on, and it was lost forever. Totally frustrating, right? For this program to work correctly, I have to have a constant Internet connection. Stay with me here. I want to make a conscious effort to renew my mind, to refresh my screen so to speak. But I also want my relationship with God to be so close and personal that He continually renews my mind. I want to choose a path, a pattern of behavior, a habitual lifestyle of submission to Him, so that I am constantly connected and He is constantly renewing my mind. We are pleasing to God; we avoid conforming to the world when we allow God to work continually in our lives through an ongoing relationship. We communicate with Him, and He with us, through His Word and through prayer and meditation on His word. As I stopped to contemplate this thought, I noticed the statement on my screen that said "all changes saved to drive." Another profound thought. When we meditate on and contemplate what He has taught us and what He has done in our lives, the changes He makes in our lives are made more permanent. We are ready to add more positive changes to our lives. We become increasingly pleasing in His sight.

What is necessary for us to be living sacrifices, pleasing to God?

Humility, recognition of our sinfulness, and faith that God is true to His promises are necessary for us to be living sacrifices. We are to think of ourselves with sober judgment. In light of God's righteousness, we must see our own sinful state. It is a sobering thought and can be life changing if we truly recognize the significance of our unworthiness. This can't be a half=hearted recognition. One of our children, when he was in high school, was stopped coming home from baseball practice going 95 miles per hour in a 55 mile per hour zone. At that moment he clearly recognized his transgression, and thereafter controlled his speed in the car more carefully. However, this knowledge didn't generalize to other areas of his life. Not long after that, he was with some other teenagers who had marijuana in their possession. He did not, thankfully, but was there when the police arrived. That scared him, and to the best of my knowledge, he avoided that crowd of friends after that. But he continued to make other bad choices: tobacco, alcohol, taking my credit card without my knowledge, staying out late. He only addressed one transgression at a time. We can't do that with God. We must look at our own sinful condition with sober judgment and accept Him by faith.

Read Romans 14:17-19

In context, Paul is talking about being supportive of those with weaker faith. In those days there were pagan religions that believed that the eating of meat sacrificed to idols caused the spirit of that god to become part of the person consuming the meat. Some of the early believers were still caught up in that mindset and fearful of eating meat purchased in the market because it could possibly have been sacrificed to an idol. He is encouraging the believers to avoid anything that would cause someone else to stumble.

Eating and drinking are important parts of any society, not just for nutrition and health, but also for fellowship and conversation. My husband has diabetes, and we have tried just about every lifestyle change diet available to address his blood sugar. Admittedly, I was fanatically committed to whatever food track we were taking at the time. In retrospect, some of them were just weird. But even the times that we ate only textured vegetable protein as a meat substitute, ground our own grain, avoided dairy, etc., we still brought our own food to our church Wednesday night meals because the fellowship was important. Sharing meals has been a part of human culture since Adam and Eve. For the early Christians, the issue of meat sacrificed to idols caused a break in that fellowship for some of the believers. Paul wanted them to know that food was not the issue. Righteousness, peace and joy in the Spirit are the characteristics that please God, and additionally receive human approval. When our hearts and lives are made righteous through God's Spirit in us, when we have peace and joy in the Spirit, we are pleasant company to others. Not only are we pleasing to God, we are a witness to others and an encouragement to fellow believers.

Read 2 Corinthians 2: 14-17

I am extremely sensitive to smells. I can walk through the mall and smell if someone is wearing raw silk. I can walk into a building and know if there is a mouse somewhere in the building. Several years ago, we lived in an older parsonage. The bottom floor was our home. The upstairs was completely closed off from the first floor and had an outside staircase. It was used for Sunday School classrooms. I kept telling my husband that there was a gas leak in our house. He didn't smell it, but because I was so persistent, he asked some others to come smell. They all thought I was imagining things. However, quite by accident and several months into my concern about a gas leak, they found a pinhole gas leak inside a wall in the upstairs restroom. I could smell something that in my mind was very dangerous. (Funny story here: I was rocking our baby, who was peacefully asleep in my arms. I must have dozed off a little too, but was apparently worried about that gas leak. This home was near an Air Force base and we would frequently have planes fly over our house. This particular day, there was a sonic boom. My first thought was that the gas leak had caused the house to explode. I jumped straight up and out of the chair, waking the baby up.) That gas leak was an aroma of death to me, and a warning to others of its danger. Conversely, some smells give us a sense of peace. When I was a child, we had a gardenia bush right by our front door. My daddy took very good care of that shrub, even building a frame and covering it with a quilt when a hard freeze was predicted. I was Daddy's little girl. He would bring me flowers from that gardenia bush. I have a potted gardenia on my back porch. I can pick one of those gardenias and a feeling of peace and calm comes over me. I suddenly feel very loved, no matter what other circumstances I face.

Our sense of smell is directly connected to areas of our brain that produce strong feelings and memories. God's choice of the word "aroma" seems significant to me because of that neural pathway. (Fifth Sense) When we spread the aroma of Christ, the response in others is deeply felt. For the lost it is the aroma of death, which we pray will lead them to life in Christ. To other believers, and most importantly to God, it is the aroma of life. This is not something that we can fake. Paul reminds the Christians at Corinth that he spoke sincerely to them about Christ Jesus. I have purchased gardenia perfume, gardenia candles, gardenia lotion, etc. But none of those fabricated smells give me the same feelings of love, peace and calm that the real gardenia flowers do. It is the same way with the aroma of Christ. The aroma we have must truly come from Him. We cannot pretend to have the aroma of Christ. We have heard the saying, "You can fool some of the people all of the time, and all of the people some of the time, but you can't fool all the people all the time." Remember, we can never deceive God. He knows our hearts better than we do ourselves.

Read Hebrews 13:20-21

How are we equipped to be pleasing to God?

When Jesus sacrificed Himself and resurrected by His mighty power, He fulfilled the covenant He had instituted before time began. His sacrifice made it possible for us to accept His gift of salvation and allow Him to work in us. Then He equips us with everything we need to do His will and please Him. God does not ask us to do anything that He does not equip us to do. Being in God's will and doing God's will are possible when He works in us and equips us.

BEARING FRUIT IN EVERY GOOD WORK

Read Psalm 92: 12-15

The place where we now live is part of the property that was homesteaded by my great-great-grandfather. Part of our yard was the home place of my great-great-uncle Andrew (Ander). We didn't notice this when we started clearing the property to make it our yard, but there are five huge persimmon trees around Uncle Ander's place. That means those trees have been there since the late 1800s. They begin to produce fruit in the Spring but before harvest time in the Fall, all the fruit falls off. We haven't been able to use any of the fruit. That is pretty frustrating to see the trees covered heavily with fruit and then not see any of it harvested. I don't know anything about the care of persimmon trees, but I'm sure there is some way to prune or fertilize that will help the fruit mature. Just because we have been Christians for years doesn't mean we are producing good fruit. I wonder if God looks at our fruit, or lack thereof, and is frustrated with us for not flourishing in His courts. I want to be productive all of my days on this earth. I want my commitment to God to stay fresh.

God also wants us to continue to produce fruit after many years of following Him, and He knows exactly the formula for that to happen. We must be planted in the house of the Lord. What does that mean? One of the characteristics of a plant is that it stays where the gardener, or nature, puts it. It doesn't get up and move around. This is particularly true when it has a good root system. This Spring I tried to transplant a climbing vine. When I started to dig up the roots to do this, the root system was so large I didn't think I was physically capable of lifting it from its spot and moving it to another, so I did not transplant it from the place where it was firmly established. When we are planted and rooted in Christ, in the house of the Lord, we are not easily moved away from Him to a place of unproductiveness, apathy, or false teaching. To continue to produce fruit, we must be unmovable from our place with God.

We must also be well nourished or we will not continue to grow and produce fruit. I recently transplanted some marigolds and costus plants that were in hanging baskets. The root system had become so large that the baskets could not contain them. They were not receiving adequate water and nutrients. If I didn't water them multiple times a day, they would shrivel up and wilt. They were top heavy and the baskets were tilting sideways. I planted them out in the yard where they could spread their roots, have adequate moisture and nutrients, have the stability to support them, and could continue to grow. When we are planted in the house of the Lord where we are rooted in Him, then we are nourished by His word, His Spirit sustains and supports us, and we continue to grow and produce fruit.

Read Jeremiah 17:7-8

In whom do you place your confidence, to always be there for you, to encourage you to be the person you should be?

One of the young ladies who came to my house for Bible study was a single expectant mother. She was emotionally needy, and I misinterpreted that as spiritual seeking. She became very dependent on me, and even though she lived with her mother, she asked that I be with her in the delivery room. She called me in the wee hours of the morning to drive her to the hospital. During labor the doctors determined that she would need a C-section and wheeled her into surgery. While I was waiting for her to return, I received a call from my son that my daughter-in-law had severe, life-threatening preeclampsia and was being air-flighted to a larger hospital for an emergency C-section. Our grandson would be born at 28 weeks gestation. I waited for my young friend to return with her baby and explained that I would be leaving the next day to be with my son and daughter in law. In my mind that should have been perfectly logical. She had her mother with her and a perfectly healthy baby. Our sweet baby weighed in at 2 pounds 8 ounces and was in the NICU. This young lady had apparently placed her confidence in me rather than in God, was very angry with me, and never returned to Bible study again. I wanted God to use me to minister to these young ladies in Bible study. But when she placed her confidence in me, I let her down. Any human on the face of the earth will let you down if you place your confidence in them. Your mother will let you down. Your father will let you down. Your spouse will let you down. Your children will let you down. Your pastor will let you down. Your best friend will let you down. The only One worthy of your confidence is God. He never fails you.

What happens in our lives when we put our confidence in God?

Regardless of the circumstances, we have no fear. We do not worry. We continue to produce fruit.

I would have classified my mother as a worrier. She was a "hand-wringer." She was one of the most selfless people I have ever known, but it was obvious when she was concerned about some circumstances in the lives of those she loved. She hardly ever said anything but she quietly rubbed her hands together. When she was diagnosed with terminal pancreatic cancer, she never showed any signs of worry. She continued to minister to those in her church family and to us. Two weeks before she died, our son had an emergency appendectomy. She and my daddy drove four hours to keep our other children so we could be at the hospital with him. Almost as soon as they returned home, she was hospitalized with massive internal bleeding. As the blood slowly filled her chest and caused her to be unable to take in enough breath to speak, she asked for paper and pen to write. She wrote each of us notes asking us to take care of each other. Her oncologist told us that he had never seen a patient die with such peace and dignity. Even though I would have thought of her as a worrier, when she faced the eventuality of her own death, she had complete confidence in God and continued to bear fruit.

Read John 15: 1-8

I am trying to grow grapes and muscadines. I know that in order to bear good fruit, the vines have to be pruned so that there is one main branch. In theory, that sounds easy enough to do. I can't seem to manage that. My vines are a tangled mess. I am learning that it takes a true gardener to know how to prune effectively to produce grapes and muscadines. God is the Master Gardener. He knows exactly how to prepare (prune) us to bear fruit.

Based on John 15: 1-8, explain the requirements and the process of bearing much good fruit.

We become a part of the vine when we acknowledge our sinfulness, repent, and accept Christ's gift of salvation. We are clean when we receive the Word of God in Christ. We recognize that we are powerless to produce good fruit without Him. We are aware that we face temptations to continue to sin, and that we must submit to God to protect us and deliver us from those temptations. We allow Him to take away the "branches" that sap our spiritual strength, those worldly entanglements that keep us from being productive. When this happens, God is glorified and we bear fruit, serving as a testimony to others that God is indeed the Master Gardener, and drawing others to also submit to Him for salvation and spiritual productiveness.

Read Romans 7:4 fruit for God.

According to Romans 7:4, why were we saved?

Prior to accepting Christ, we belonged to our sinfulness, which was made evident through the law. Through Christ's sacrificial death and resurrection, we belong to Him so that we will bear fruit. When we think of something belonging to us, we own that item, place, or animal. (My grammar geek is coming out. We own that noun-person, place, thing.) We are responsible for its safe keeping, nourishment, and well-being. Then whatever product results from that item also belongs to us and should serve to benefit us in some way, whether economic, aesthetic, physical or emotional. When we belonged to sinfulness, we had a bad owner who did not care for our well-being. The fruit we produced was useless or destructive. Now that we belong to Christ, we are well tended and capable, not through our own abilities, but through His, to produce fruit for Him.

GROWING IN THE KNOWLEDGE OF GOD

Read Ephesians 4:11-16

What does this scripture tell us about the purpose for which God gave the spiritual gifts?

What are the roles of apostle, prophet, evangelist, pastor and teacher?

What should be the result when they fulfill their roles?

My husband's great uncle, and namesake, was a leader in a "church" which I strongly believe preaches and teaches doctrines contrary to scripture. His belief in this false theology blinded him to the truth of God's redemption. When trials came into his life, he was tossed about. When his wife died, he declared himself to be an atheist and died without a relationship with Christ. This is an extreme example. As heartbreaking as this scenario is, an equally concerning situation exists in our churches today. Whether because of lack of solid, Biblical teaching or because of lack of commitment from individuals, many people who attend church regularly are tossed about by all kinds of false teaching. I personally believe it is both. Church members, Christians, do not grow to maturity. Some are fully committed to their church, serving tirelessly. Yet, they believe all kinds of myths and speculations to be scriptural. Recently, one of my social media "friends" posted a particularly egregious departure from what the scripture says. I felt compelled to address this sort of post in a generalized comment about being sure that what we post on social media is scriptural. When I saw her the next Sunday at church, she asked me if my post was about something she had posted. I failed to address the issue with her. I responded with a lie that I didn't remember whose post had prompted me to make my comment. I should have addressed it with her but I was weak. (There was at least a half truth in my statement because many of my friends post unscriptural things on social media. I am not even entirely sure that I am innocent in this. We just repost things that look pretty or sound cute.) If you are honest, you may have been in similar situations. This scripture tells us that we should speak the truth in love. I failed to speak the truth to this lady. And the sad part is that she is in her eighties. How many other people through the years have also failed to speak the truth in love to her? Let's not focus on the bad news though. What happens if we do obey and apply the principles in this scripture? We are taught sound doctrine. We, like the Bereans, search the scriptures for ourselves to see if what we are being taught is scriptural.

Read Acts 17:11

When we are fully committed to following and obeying Christ in all things, we grow to maturity. We work together as part of His body, the church, to fulfill both the evangelistic and discipleship components of the Great Commission (Matthew 28:18-20.). In turn new believers are taught, commit, grow and complete the circle. Envision that. How amazing is God's plan!

Read 1 Peter 2:2

Unless there is a health problem, most babies are born hungry. They desire milk almost immediately after birth. Our oldest grandson was born nearly 3 months premature. He was not strong enough to seek out milk on his own. Making sure he had adequate nutrition was a major part of the treatment he received in the NICU.

We all know how important nutrition is to physical growth and health. The same is true of our spiritual growth. When we are reborn through Christ, we need spiritual nourishment to grow. We desire to know more about Him through reading and studying His word, and to know Him better by spending time with Him in prayer and meditation. (Please bear with me as I may be stretching an analogy here, but I think there is a point to be made.) God is our Father in this new birth. The church as His bride has a shared responsibility to nurture us, as a mother would her newborn baby. Then we begin to develop the ability to obtain nourishment for ourselves. Some of the first words a baby learns are directly related to this concept. "Mama" is definitely associated with both love and food. Then words like "milk", "bite", "baba" (bottle), "cookie", "more", etc. come early in their vocabulary development. The church, our fellow believers in whatever type of group we have, initially provides us with teaching and support, but as we grow stronger and more mature, we should begin to find that spiritual food for ourselves. Many mothers, myself included, have found small children finding food sources for themselves in quite comical places: sitting on the pantry floor eating peanut butter out of the jar with their fingers, digging petrified food out of the couch cushions, sitting on the kitchen counter eating dry oatmeal, hiding peanut butter crackers in their drawers to save for later. If we are growing "normally" spiritually, we will begin to feed ourselves and not depend entirely on others for that nourishment. Like newborn babies, grow. That's simple enough.

Do you have a hunger for God?

Read 2 Peter 3:17-18

God forewarns us because He wants us to know ahead of time that there are those who would lead us astray. He wants us to grow to maturity. If we are taken captive by false teachings, then we will not understand what it means to be completely committed to Christ Jesus, and will not grow in His grace and knowledge. There was a time when children walked or rode bicycles around their communities without fear. When I was a child, my friends and I put a brown bag lunch in the basket of our bicycles and rode around our small town from breakfast to supper. Nobody warned us of "stranger danger." I don't know if the danger was there, and we were all unaware of it, or if evil has grown that significantly. Parents now begin early in their child's life to warn them not to talk to strangers, because they know that children are by nature generally trusting. When our son was young, we were shopping in our local big box store. He struck up a conversation with a man (I'm confident my son started the conversation because that is his personality.) I noticed the conversation and joined it. After he left the store, I reminded my son about talking to strangers. He responded, "He's not a stranger. His name is Bob." (The usual way my son started a conversation with someone he didn't know was "Hi. My name's Caleb. What's yours?" so based on his definition of "stranger", there was no such thing.) God warns us of the danger, but sometimes we either don't heed His warnings, or don't understand what the warning means. We put ourselves in spiritual danger. In order to be aware of the danger, we need to be growing in Him. Without a clear knowledge-base we don't recognize what is false teaching and what is spiritual danger. My son wasn't purposely being disobedient. He honestly thought that if you knew someone's name, they weren't a stranger. Immature Christians are like children. They trust anyone who says that they are Christian. Just because people carry something that looks like a Bible, or have a television show with a pulpit and pews, or write a book or have a social media page that uses the name of Christ, people believe what they say. This is just as wrong as my son believing that Bob wasn't a stranger because he knew his name. As Christians, if we don't understand the danger, we cannot avoid it. And again, it is a growing circle. If we grow in Him, we understand the danger and avoid it, making it possible for us to continue on the true path because we are not led astray to follow that which is false and spiritually dangerous.

STRENGTHENED WITH ALL POWER, AS HE ENABLES US:

ACCORDING TO HIS GLORIOUS MIGHT

When God appeared to Abraham, He identified Himself as God Almighty, *El-Shaddai*.

Read Genesis 17:1

The dictionary (New Oxford Dictionary) defines "almighty" as having complete power. Early in scripture, God established that He is all-powerful, having complete power in all things. Recognizing this characteristic (attribute) of God is central to our willingness to submit to Him wholeheartedly. Abraham fell face down when he recognized that he was in the presence of God Almighty.

What does it mean to be strengthened according to <u>His</u> glorious might?

We are fascinated with the strong, powerful, and exceptional among us. Little boys' closets and toy chests are often full of action figures, whether superheroes, soldiers, wrestlers, football players, or robots. In popular action movies the characters use their ability to strategize, their strength, and their skill to defeat the enemy. Entire television networks are devoted to sports. Absolutely none of these people, whether flesh and blood, or fictional characters can ever compare to the glorious might of God. Think for a minute about how we as believers fully committed to following Him can be strengthened according to His power.

ENDURANCE

We often think of endurance in the context of suffering through unpleasant circumstances. When my daddy was 82 years old, he went with our church on a Senior Adult trip to Gatlinburg, Tennessee. He loved beautiful scenery, and traveling, but he did not like country music. He hated being at the first show, and seemed miserable. So, when we were about to go to the second show, I asked if he would rather stay at the motel, and he did. But, when it was time for the third show, he said that he wanted to go with us. I reminded him that it was country music. He said, "I can endure anything for a short while." In this context, enduring something was tolerating a form of music which was not his preference.

Athletes want to build their endurance in order to perform at peak performance in a strenuous task. Our older son had wanted to play football from the time he was a toddler. When he was in high school, he set out to increase his endurance. At that time, we lived on a rather steep hill on a busy street. Somewhere, he obtained a large tractor tire, which he attached to a chain and pulled up and down this hill. I can only imagine what people thought as they drove by and saw him pulling this tractor tire up the sidewalk. He was either oblivious to the absurdity of this, or was so focused on his goal that he didn't care. As comical as this is, he was wholeheartedly committed to building his endurance.

Spiritual endurance has deeper meaning, and greater significance than enduring an unpleasant experience or gaining physical prowess. My father was willing to suffer through the music, and my son was willing to make a spectacle of himself, as well as stretch his physical limits. Both these required only human effort. The process of developing spiritual endurance will involve suffering, stretching our limits, and commitment. But this is not accomplished through our own effort. Spiritual endurance is the result of yielding to Christ's work in us.

Read Romans 15: 3-6.

Based on Romans 15: 3-6, how do we gain endurance?

What are the results of spiritual endurance?

Spiritual endurance requires a commitment to study the scriptures. This passage tells us that two of the purposes of the written word are to teach us endurance and encourage us. In the midst of suffering, in the stretching of our spiritual limits, in yielding in wholehearted commitment, God's Word encourages us to endure whatever hardships or trials we face. When we commit to studying His Word, God works in us to give us endurance and encourage us. The result is a Christlikeness in us and a bond with other believers that is possible only through the indwelling of His Spirit and results in glory to God, and not to ourselves.

Read 2 Corinthians 1: 3-11

How does God use the circumstances of our lives, whether pleasant or unpleasant, to develop endurance in us?

How does He use what we have experienced to develop endurance in others?

Paul experienced multiple life-threatening encounters with various mobs, Jewish leaders, and Roman authorities. Believers in some places around the world today also experience martyrdom for the sake of Christ Jesus. Here in the United States, we seldom experience this type of persecution.

Our sufferings are often personal but seemingly unbearable. When our oldest daughter was a junior in college, she told us that she wasn't coming home for Thanksgiving break because she was spending the holiday with her roommate's family. While disappointed, we did not realize the significance. The week after Thanksgiving break, we received a call from the Dean of Students telling us that neither our daughter nor her roommate had returned from break, and asking if we knew where they were. We had no idea. This was the beginning of an emotional roller coaster of epic proportions, which lasted for years. We made mistakes in trying to deal with the situation. But this was also one of the most spiritually enlightening times of my life. Even now, it is difficult to formulate a way to express what we learned during this experience. Through the Old Testament prophecies, God gave me a glimpse of how He views my sin and rebellion. He has a complicated mix of anger over our sin and unfailing love for us. Through the parable of the prodigal son, He taught me the importance of true repentance, and that He does not force us to come back to Him. He waits eagerly for our return and is ready to welcome us with open arms. I prayed that God would do whatever it took to bring her back, even to the point of the death of her family members. He gave me a new understanding of His willingness to sacrifice Himself for us. We were able to endure this trial only because we came to realize the great lessons that He was teaching us and to accept the comfort only He can provide. What we saw happening over the following years was that He put people in our path who were experiencing similar trials to those we had experienced and who were seeking some sort of comfort, guidance, and understanding. God has used our suffering to comfort and teach others. (She now lives across the road from us. She completed her doctorate and now teaches at a university near our home. She is a great help to us in many ways.) Learning and developing endurance is not easy or pleasant. It is difficult. Would I have chosen this journey? Absolutely not. Am I grateful for God's Presence through these trials and thankful for the lessons I learned? Without a doubt. When we commit to growing spiritually, when we allow Him to work in our lives, we develop endurance for future trials as God prepares us for His ministry to others.

Read Psalm 112:6-9

According to Psalm 112: 6-9, what is it that endures forever?

We have discussed the effects endurance has on us in dealing with suffering and trials. In these verses the focus of endurance changes somewhat. The righteousness of the righteous is what endures. We know that we are incapable of righteousness on our own. As I thoughtfully read this verse, I am struck with a confused emotion. When I received a phone call from the hospital that my husband had been in an accident, I calmly made the necessary arrangements. I was 6 hours away from him, because I was doing some yearly work on our cabin. The call came about 9:00 p.m., the time I was expecting him to arrive at home after hugging me goodbye that afternoon. The hospital would not give me any details. I calmly called my son, who lived about an hour from our cabin, and arranged for him to drive with me to the hospital. I then called our youth minister and asked him to preach the next morning. Next, I called my other children to let them know. Then I called my police officer brother-in-law to see if he could use his connections to find out any information. Completely calm and organized. I had no visible fear. I didn't even feel fear. I had it under control. But years later, I am beginning to question whether my righteousness has endured. Don't get me wrong, I have not rejected God. But I can't honestly say that I haven't felt shaken, that I have always felt secure, that I have been steadfast. My enemies have been the enemies that have attacked my husband: cancer, diabetes related complications, and anxiety and sleeplessness. My personal enemies have been bitterness, anger, and a changing view of my husband. This battle has gone on for years, and I see no victory in sight, at least when I look through human eyes. So, how does my righteousness endure when the enemy seems daunting and I am weak? Through faith, repentance, and dependence on God. I cannot endure by my own effort. You cannot endure by your own effort. Only through dependence on God can our righteousness endure.

Think of times when your righteousness was tested but endured through dependence on God.

RIGHTEOUSNESS

Read Psalm 143:2

For our righteousness to endure, we must first have some sort of righteousness. I have students who have difficulty obeying the rules at school. Honestly, they have difficulty controlling their behavior in any situation. In many cases, there is a reasonable explanation for this. Their parents, and I use the most generic definition of that term, have used drugs prior to their birth and in their presence now, abused them, failed to care for them, or other atrocities which we cannot even imagine. In other cases, there is some chromosomal mutation that affects the child. For the purpose of discussion, let's equate their inability to follow social norms with our ability to be righteous. Stay with me here. I talked to the classroom teacher of one of these children yesterday. We both talked about how much we love that child, but how difficult it is to make significant headway in changing his behavior. The day before, he had struggled all day long. When he was with me for speech therapy, he picked at a nearly healed blister on his finger until it was bleeding enough that I felt like I needed to suspend therapy and take him to the nurse. She said that he had picked through several layers of skin. This seemed to be a purposeful act on his part. He knew he wasn't supposed to do that but did it to avoid the work he needed to do. He lost reward points in the classroom, in addition to many points he had lost earlier in the day. He told his teacher that he was going to be good the rest of the day. When he came back from his class's time in the library, the librarian bragged about him to the teacher. He was good for that particular 30 minutes. He was trying to have a righteousness of his own. But that righteousness could not endure. It wasn't long before he was disruptive and disrespectful in the classroom. He could not do it on his own. We can't either. Teachers have pretty high standards, but God's standards are even higher. No human, not even one, is capable of living up to His standards. We cannot obtain righteousness on our own.

Take a moment to acknowledge to God your inability to be righteous.

Read Romans 3:10-18

The only way to have righteousness is through accepting Christ as your Lord and Savior. This scripture is clear. We are incapable of righteousness. I won't talk about all these descriptions of our righteousness, but I want to share one that is very sad, but a good illustration. We had not seen one of our outside dogs for a few days. We live on the farm, with no leash laws. Our dogs are a large breed who were bred centuries ago to protect the flocks, so they are very territorial and often spend time with the cows in the pasture. We weren't overly concerned, because he could have just been hanging out with the cattle. Our cats are also pretty good at going out into the pasture and bringing us gifts (dead rodents) to the back porch. I started to smell an unpleasant smell. Initially, I thought it was a dead rodent under the porch. The smell continued to get worse. My husband texted me at work to tell me he found the dog in the corral area with his head stuck in a large plastic jar. He had apparently suffocated because he couldn't get his head out. (I was very sad, but I also thought how foolish he was to stick his head in a jar, and how different the situation would have been if dogs had thumbs.) His body had reached the point that we could not pick him up to bury him without him falling apart. We had to have a sort of improvised cremation. The point is that even though he was a very good dog, he was full of decay and had an obnoxious odor. That describes how God sees our righteousness. We need Him. His ability to change that horrible smell of spiritual death into newness of life is beyond our understanding. Yet when we accept Him by faith, he makes us a new creation.

If you have not accepted His gift, please acknowledge your sinfulness now, repent (turn away) from your sin, and accept His gift of salvation. If you have questions about this, please talk to a Christian friend and ask them to explain this to you.

Read Romans 3:22-24

Even though we have absolutely no righteousness of our own, we are freely given salvation by His grace. When we acknowledge our sinfulness, repent and accept His freely given gift, our sin is forgiven. That gift will endure, not because of our goodness, but because of His love for us. Look at the promises listed in Psalm 112.

Read Psalm 112:6-9

What results does the psalmist list in Psalm 112: 6-9 to describe God's work in the life of a believer?

We will never lose that gift of salvation because we have been made righteous through Jesus' sacrifice; we are not saved by our own efforts. Then, because of Jesus' work in us, the results in our lives are evident. We will never be shaken. We have no fear of bad news. Our trust in the Lord is steadfast.

PATIENCE

Our second child was about 2 years old when we were standing in the checkout line at the grocery store behind a particularly impatient customer. My son observed for a few minutes, then quoting a cartoon (Butler) about an unsuspecting character who substitute taught in a class of unruly students, looked at the man and said, "You just gotta have patience, man." I thought it was hilarious, but I'm not sure how the man felt about it. Our world is full of impatience. With God's Spirit working in us, we are called to be different. We have received God's patience, and are in turn to show patience to others.

Read 1 Timothy 1:15-16

How does Christ Jesus display His immense patience in us?

We are back to prepositions again; He shows patience <u>toward</u> us and <u>in</u> us, <u>with</u> us and <u>through</u> us. See the pattern here. Scripture is clear that He is patient <u>with</u> us, wanting us all to come to repentance. (2 Peter 3:9) He is patient <u>toward</u> us, willing to forgive our sin when we confess to Him. (1 John 1:9) But as a result of His Holy Spirit dwelling <u>in</u> us, He shows patience to others <u>through</u> us. He uses His patience toward us and in us to draw others to Himself.

JOY

I have heard it said that there is significance in the number of times scripture addresses a certain topic. In the New International Version, there are 242 references to joy. That is pretty significant. The topic of joy is multi-dimensional. From the character of God Himself, to the effect His presence has on us, to our emotion when we see His work in others. When I try to think of wonderful examples of joyful hearts in the face of not such wonderful circumstances, the list seems short. A sweet Christian friend's son either accidentally shot himself, or committed suicide. I honestly don't know which. The police report said it was accidental. His mother believes it was purposeful. Even with that belief in her heart, she faced his death with joy in her heart. Her response to horrible circumstances was and is a testimony to others of the joy of the Lord.

However, the list of people who "Aren't happy unless they're unhappy" seems much longer. Why is that? I'm not pointing fingers at anyone except myself, but is the number of people in each category backwards because we don't have a strong committed relationship with Christ?

Does the Joy of the Lord fill your life, in the good and the not so good?

CHAPTER 6

POWER IN RELATIONSHIP

HIS PRESENCE

The presence of God results in great joy and worship.

Read Leviticus 9:24

God's presence is not all warm fuzzies. He is Consuming Fire. Yes, He is Love, but He is also Judgment. There would have been no need for Jesus' sacrificial death had God not been righteous, just and holy, and had we not been deserving of His wrath. In this scripture, fire came out from the presence of the Lord and consumed the offerings. On the day of Pentecost, tongues of fire touched the disciples and filled them with His Spirit. The last few words of Leviticus 9:24 intrigue me. They shouted for joy and fell facedown. In my finite mind, these two actions seem contradictory, but they are not. Imagine being aware of the presence of the Lord, seeing fire come out of what the human eye could see only as thin air, and consume an animal completely. Without the understanding of what was happening that would be terrifying. The primal reaction would be to run. But with the knowledge of who God is, the terror would elicit worship and humbling of ourselves. Think now about what this holy fire did. Fire consumed the offering, the sacrifice, the symbol of repentance and forgiveness. Joy! Joy that sin is forgiven. Worship! Worship of The Holy God evidenced by All Consuming Fire.

Read Psalm 16:11

With overwhelming joy, we acknowledge that God the Holy Consuming Fire loves us, and fellowships with us. He makes his presence known to His children as comfort, love, and joy. We have pleasure in His presence. Interestingly, I don't always feel His presence. Faith is so important. Trust that He is with us. I admit, sometimes, the commitment to spend time alone with Him is an effort. Some mornings when I sit here on this couch, I have difficulty focusing on Him. But I know by faith that His Spirit is always with me. Always. And this is my comfort, my joy, my pleasure. He will never leave me. Yes, there are times when I feel His presence in my time alone with Him.

But God's presence with us is not based on our emotional response, but rather on His faithfulness and our faith. When we base God's presence on the things that cause our amygdala and limbic system (Chemistry of Emotions) to elicit emotions in us, we can quickly forget the who of Who He is. God's presence is based on His promises. The world defines as pleasurable things that result in these chemical and neurological reactions. Spiritual pleasure is an act of faith.

Read Psalm 51:11-12

David had committed adultery, lied, then conspired to commit murder to conceal his adultery. The prophet Nathan confronted him. David was deeply repentant and wrote this psalm as a prayer. His heartfelt prayer was that God would not cast him from His presence. He asked God to restore the joy of His salvation. Look at the pronouns. David prayed "restore the joy of <u>YOUR</u> salvation" (emphasis mine). David recognized that salvation was God's alone and provided to him and to us as a gift by grace through faith. The joy of that true salvation had been masked by his sinfulness. Perhaps he had viewed Joab as his savior when he sent Uriah to the battle front then withdrew the rest of the army without telling Uriah. This meant certain death for Uriah and temporarily covered David's sin. Whatever the case, David had shifted the focus of his faith away from God and lost the joy of God's salvation and His presence. David knew that only could God cover his sin. He could not cleanse or conceal his own sin. However, he turned to Joab and a devious plan rather than to God. I have heard, and perhaps used, the words "savior" and "salvation" loosely and irreverently. Several years ago, I read about a celebrity making a speech about a newly elected public official, calling him "our savior". We use the terms lightly to describe someone who has fixed our lawnmower, provided much needed documents, or brought us ice cream when we are sick. Recognizing the uniqueness of God's provision of His salvation is key to the joy we have in His presence. Once again, the joy of His presence is not based on our emotional response but hinges on repentant faith and absolute trust in the only Savior.

Think about the times you have placed your trust in someone or something other than God. Did you have joy in His presence then? What lessons did you learn from that experience? (I freely admit that some of us may be in this state, even as we contemplate this scripture. Acknowledge that and pray in repentance.)

IN HIS LOVE

Read Psalm 90:14

Where do we even begin to comment on God's unfailing love! Contemplate even the word itself. Unfailing. Recently we have watched the national news as floods, earthquakes, hurricanes, and tornadoes have devastated and destroyed sound, solid structures. Bridges that were designed by gifted engineers and constructed by committed workers have broken and are no longer passable. Well built homes and buildings are no longer inhabitable. Nothing we know on this earth is unfailing. But God's love is unfailing through all eternity. And not only is His love unfailing, His love is satisfying.

HIS BLESSINGS

Read Deuteronomy 16:13-15

God wants us to recognize the blessings he has bestowed on us, and to have <u>complete</u> joy. For parents and professionals who work with children with severe disabilities, celebrating the small steps becomes a lifestyle. Several years ago, I made home visits to work with children with disabilities and to help their parents learn how to work with them as well. One of these children was a three-year-old with Down syndrome. While not all parents were amazing at working with the children, his were. They were fully committed to doing whatever they needed to do for him. And more importantly, they were fully committed to Jesus as their Savior and worked tirelessly in His name to minister to others. This child had a very limited vocabulary of single word utterances. One day as his mother and I sat on the floor working with him, he put two words together. "Want car." We celebrated the harvest that God had provided us! I have a student now who has trouble transitioning from one activity to another. That manifests itself by stomping his feet, loudly expressing his disdain for whatever task he is expected to do next, refusing to walk down the hallway, falling down into the floor, leaning against the wall when walking down the hallway, etc. A few weeks ago, perhaps because he is maturing or because I figured out a strategy, (I should say that God showed me a strategy) he walked calmly down the hallway to therapy, did all his work, and walked calmly back to his classroom. I could hardly contain my joy! In other words, I had trouble walking calmly down the hallway because I wanted to jump and skip with joy! Sometimes we become greedy in our harvest expectations. Granted, sometimes God gives us huge harvests. But sometimes, he gives us our harvests in smaller increments. The key is that we recognize these harvests and celebrate with joy.

Think about the harvests that God has provided you. Give him the glory for the things we often claim as harvests we have produced by ourselves. Write some of them and celebrate with joy that He has blessed you with these harvests.

HIS WORK IN OTHERS THROUGH US

Read 1 Chronicles 29:16-18

Several years ago, a dear couple from our church had traveled to Kenya, Africa on a mission trip with a relative's church. While there, they became familiar with a non-governmental organization that ministered to young unwed, widowed, or abandoned mothers and their children. These young women had very few rights and protections. They lived in the slums in conditions that those of us who live in the United States cannot even comprehend unless we have seen it ourselves. While I understand that this is not the official position of their government, the culture in that area leaves few options for this population. The stated purpose of this organization was to teach these young women skills that they could use to support themselves and their children. They also provided a school/preschool for the children. They did all this in a small three-bedroom house without running water. A group of people in our church, after prayer and consultation with experts, determined to purchase land for this ministry to build a more suitable structure to house their training program and preschool/school. We set a goal and announced what we knew was an ambitious amount in a limited time. One person after another contacted my husband to give checks equal to an average year's wages for many in our country. The fundraising goal was exceeded. The vision of this one couple continued to grow. While our daughter was in college, she spent two summers living and working with this ministry. I have made two trips to work with these women. When we moved to another church in another state, our church there caught the vision and raised the money to help provide running water and participate in building the new facility. Our friends quit their jobs and moved to Kenya for three years to volunteer to serve God there. What joy we all have when we look back at what God can do through people who are willing to serve and give sacrificially.

Can you think of a time when a group of people have made tremendous personal sacrifices because of the example of someone who had a heart to minister? Praise God for the joy you felt in that. Maybe you haven't experienced anything like this. If you are willing, pray that God will open your eyes to ways He wants you to serve and give sacrificially.

Read 2 Corinthians 7:3-4

I am not typically a bold person. Several years ago, I was having a pretty intense conversation with two friends. Actually, I was mostly listening. One of the friends was very timid and quiet in dealing with significant issues that needed to be addressed. The other friend had a strong personality and was not afraid to boldly address areas of conflict. We made a very odd group. The bold friend was chastising the quiet friend for not dealing with the issue forcefully. She told her she was too quiet. In her effort to defend herself against this accusation, she said "Mary Lynne's quiet too!" The bold friend replied, "She's not quiet. She's reserved." Hey! I'm sitting right here! So, I can't really identify with Paul's frankness in dealing with the Christians in Corinth. To put his statement in context, he had previously spoken harshly to them about some issues in the church which were not being addressed, specifically a man having a sexual relationship with his father's wife. Even in our tolerant and amoral society, that is frowned upon. Some things are egregious in any culture. The church had responded to his rebuke. Paul is now telling them how proud he is of them for following his instructions. Look at his expression of pride, encouragement, and joy. Paul's joy from the other believers isn't because they always did the right thing. It is because they responded to his rebuke and corrected their mistakes. We can find joy in relationships with other believers even when they have disappointed us in the past.

Are you finding joy in other believers? If not, why not? Pray now that God will restore your joy with your brothers and sisters.

Read 1 Thessalonians 1:5-7

The believers in Thessalonica were an example to other believers in the surrounding areas because of the work of the Holy Spirit. When Paul spoke the word of truth to them, God's Spirit powerfully convicted them. God used Paul to bring them to Himself as they observed how Paul and his traveling companions lived. They saw the work of God and His Spirit in them. They saw that Paul was different. They wanted to be like him and imitated him. But the reason they were an example to other believers was not because of their own efforts to imitate Paul. They were examples because they yielded themselves to the work of the Holy Spirit, just as they had seen Paul do. They made this wholehearted commitment to God in the midst of severe suffering, and were filled with joy because of God's Spirit in them. I can't help but wonder if at least part of what they saw in Paul that made them want to imitate him was his joy in the midst of suffering.

Has anyone influenced you to follow Christ completely because of the way you saw God work in them?

What was it about that person that impressed you?

Read 3 John 1:3-4

I think I can hear the tenderness in John's voice as he pens these words. Don't we all love to hear people brag about our children? John had such joy knowing that his spiritual children, those he had led to Christ and mentored in the faith, were continuing to walk faithfully in Christ Jesus. When our hearts are completely committed to Him, the influence He has through us will in turn affect others, filling us with joy because of the work He has done in them.

Think about the people who influenced you to accept Christ Jesus as your Lord. Think about those who have nourished and mentored you. Do they have great joy to see the result of God's work in you?

Think about your spiritual children. Thank God for the joy He gives you in seeing them continue to walk in the Truth.

HIS MIRACULOUS INTERVENTIONS

Read Ezra 6:22

I can truthfully say that my daughter-in-law is one of my best friends and one in whom I confide more than just about anyone. I think she feels the same way about me. She is experiencing some significant health issues right now, and I told my son that even though I didn't give birth to her, I love her like she is my own daughter. It was not always that way. We got off to a very bad start. Really bad. She would tell you the same thing. But she has such a heart for following and obeying God, and that is also my own desire. As I read the scripture above, I don't know whose attitude God changed, hers or mine. Probably both. But what has happened is a strong relationship of mutual encouragement and joy in fellowship. I rejoice and find great joy that God has worked in our relationship.

Think about a time that God has changed attitudes, yours or someone else's, and brought about a miraculous partnership. Praise him joyfully because of it.

Read Psalm 21:1

Most of us don't go onto the battlefield with weapons of war. As the mother of a soldier, I have a personal and heartfelt appreciation for those who do. As of this writing, he has spent one year in Iraq and three years in Afghanistan. Yet, the hardest battle he has fought was not against corrupt regimes or supporters of terrorism. He fought a spiritual battle, unfortunately, at the same time he was deployed. His wife wanted a big wedding, but she didn't want to be married. From the first week they were married, she would spend 3 days with him, then go "home" for 4 days. She loved alcohol and other men, and posted pictures of herself on social media obviously drunk, scantily dressed, with other men. Not only was he hurt and heart-broken because of her unfaithfulness, he was humiliated that all this was public knowledge. This went on for 3 years. We were heartbroken because we couldn't do anything to help him. We had always taught him that marriage is for one man, one woman for a lifetime. We have been married for 43 years. His grandparents were married to each other until death parted them. We watched as his joy ebbed away. He had always been the one we called "our Sunshine" and "a Barnabas" to others. We began to question whether we had taught him the principles of marriage too well. We watched as he continued to love her, forgive her, and try to hold their marriage together. Then one day, he called his dad in tears and said that he was filing for divorce. He said, "I can honestly say that I have done everything in my power to keep this marriage together." We knew this was true. I don't understand God's ways, and am hesitant to say or think that divorce is part of God's plan, but I do know that God gave the option for divorce in the case of adultery. And in His grace, He provides victories in our lives even in our weakness and sinfulness. We began to see our son return. His body had been around, but his soul had been crushed. Through a very strange situation, he began talking to a friend of his sister's friend through social media while he was in his last deployment. They talked for over a year before they met in person. This sweet Christian young lady is now our daughter-in-law.

Our son is himself again. They are involved in their church, ministering to others, and overjoyed that they will have a baby girl in 2 months. We cannot imagine how they could have even met had God not guided them together. This victory was not our sons. This victory, in the face of strong spiritual warfare, and sinfulness, was God's. We rejoice in God's victory. We know that we fight other kinds of battles and that God gives us victories in those battles. How often, though, are we so "me" centered that we see these God given victories as something we have accomplished on our own? Sometimes, it is clear that only God could have accomplished those victories. Other times, we are tempted to think we accomplished them.

Think about the times God has given victories that were clearly His. Joyfully praise Him for them.

Think back to times that you were tempted to take credit for victories that God accomplished through you. Repent if you took credit. Praise Him for those victories as well.

Read Psalm 126:2-3

When we are aware of God's miraculous workings around us, even in the unexplainable and improbable, our hearts are filled with joy. We all have our idea of our dream job. Mine was to work at an organization in our area that is considered one of the authorities on how to work with children with disabilities. Shortly after I finished my Masters in Communicative Disorders, I was working for a local public school. Since I was working with a child with some severe disabilities, I went to training to learn more about how to address her needs. I happened (by God's perfect plan) to sit next to someone who worked for my dream organization. In small talk, I asked her where she worked.

When she told me, I replied that I had always dreamed of working there. End of discussion. That night I received a phone call from the therapy coordinator at the inpatient rehabilitation program asking if I would be interested in coming for an interview. I had not applied for the job! They hired me. Six months later I was promoted to therapy coordinator. Another six months later, I was promoted to assistant administrator. And that's not even the most amazing part of this story. God opened doors for me to take several of these children to church. Evangelist David Ring (Ministries) was to speak at our church. Since many of the children at the rehab facility had cerebral palsy, I asked permission to take some to go hear him speak. If you are not familiar with him, take time to do an Internet search and listen to his testimony.

The children loved going to church. This was the unexpected beginning of an ongoing ministry. Since a handicapped accessible van can transport a limited number of children, I could not take everyone who wanted to go. We were able to take them to 3 services a week, so that as many as possible were allowed to attend. We rejoiced in seeing six children with severe disabilities and unfathomable home situations give their hearts to Jesus and follow Him in obedience through baptism. One day as I was doing speech therapy with a 12-year-old boy with a brain tumor, he said, "Mary Lynne, Can I ask you a question?" I said, "Sure. What is it?" This was his question, which by all human standards came out of the blue. "What do I have to do to go to heaven if I die?" I look back on all the improbable, and seemingly impossible things that happened in that job, and my heart is filled with joy.

What about you? What great things has God done for you? Acknowledge those with joy as you see His mighty work in and through you. Give Him praise.

BASIS OF RELATIONSHIP

HIS CHARACTER

Read 1 Chronicles 16:26-28

Joy is one part of God's multi-faceted character. He dwells in joy. Perhaps you have a visual picture in your mind of what God looks like. As indescribable as He is, I envision Him sitting on His throne majestically. And that is not wrong. It's just incomplete. He dwells in strength and joy. How do we even begin to understand that? And His Spirit indwells the believer. His joy then lives in us. My husband is a great guy, but he has a really strange sense of humor. When someone asks him how he is, he always, always, always says "Terrible." I find it unbelievably annoying. I do not understand why he thinks it's funny. When God's Spirit lives in us, His character should show through us. The world should see joy in us, not because we are healthy, or wealthy, or even happy. Joy is a characteristic of God, not an emotion. Our responsibility is to ascribe to God the Who of who He is, and acknowledge His character in all we do and all we say.

IN HIS WORD

Read Nehemiah 8:9-11

The Word of God can bring what seems to be bitter conviction of our sin, yet even in that bitterness comes great joy that God forgives and gives us strength. We had the privilege of being a part of the life of a young man with a tremendous story. His wife and child had been killed in a car accident. He had renounced the existence of God, because he could not believe that God would allow this tragedy in his life. He is a bodybuilder, and to be truthful, someone I would be afraid to meet on a dark alley. He began dating a young lady who God had allowed me to spend some time with during her own spiritual struggles. I was somewhat frightened that he would pull her away from God, because she was still fighting some spiritual battles of her own. But she was steadfast that he must come to church with her. For several weeks, he sat sullenly unresponsive to what he was hearing, but he was there. One day during the invitation, he loudly sobbed his way down the aisle and accepted Christ as His Savior. The entire congregation cried tears of joy as we witnessed this miraculous transformation. My husband had the privilege of performing the marriage ceremony for these amazing young people. We had the opportunity to spend time with this couple in their home and at sporting events. The change from anger and sullenness to joy was evident in his life and on his face. They now have children and continue to serve God faithfully. The grief of conviction of sin from God's Word filled him with a strong but temporary grief which led to a spiritual strength, much greater than the physical strength he already had, and empowers him with joy as he serves God.

Read Psalm 19:8

Since I lost the hearing in my right ear when I was 18 years old, I have had to not only make sure that my left ear faces whoever is talking to me, but also listen intently to understand what they are saying. Now to use "speech pathologist" jargon on you; the reason for this is that your language center is in the side of your brain which is opposite of your dominant side. (Wikipedia) So, since I am right hand dominant and lost the hearing in the right ear, hearing in the left ear crosses to the right side of my brain, which is not the language center. Bored yet? What that means is that I have to really listen and focus on what people are saying. To do this I subconsciously focus on their eyes. In God's amazing ways, He has used that to build relationships. What I have learned is that a person's eyes tell you much more than their words. Look at this verse again. God's commands give light to the eyes. I cannot quantify it, but I have seen it. Words may sound churchy and sincere but the eyes reveal hypocrisy. And in the face of grief and anguish, fear, pain, and confusion, the eyes reveal peace and joy when that person is walking with God. The commands and precepts of the Lord give radiance, and joy, and peace, and light to the eyes.

This is obviously not something that you can look in the mirror and see, but think for a minute. What do people see when they look into your eyes? Do they see the joyful light that the precepts and commands of the Lord give? Are you allowing God's word to change your whole being? Is God's Spirit seen in your eyes? You can't fake this. Commit now to wholeheartedly follow the commands and precepts of the Lord.

Read Psalm 119:111

When I think about my heritage, I think about my parents, grandparents and my great grandparents, people whose DNA I share and with whom I have spent time. I am so grateful that these people were a godly example to me. I saw God's work in them. Then there is the story of my great-grandfather. (I guess you could call it a funny parable.) He was a farmer. Strawberries were one of his major crops. He had always refused to do any work on Sunday out of reverence for the Lord. One year, for whatever reason, he felt it was imperative that the strawberries be harvested on Sunday. He lost his glasses while picking strawberries that day. The cost to replace his glasses was exactly the amount of money he made from the strawberries. After that, he refused to ever do any work on Sunday again. I praise God for the earthly heritage He has given me.

But I know people whose ancestors were not at all like mine. This verse doesn't say that our ancestors are our heritage. It says that God's statutes are our heritage. The most important heritage we have goes back to before time began. God is the same from eternity past to eternity future, and His statutes are our heritage. Now look at the second part of this verse (Psalm 119: 111). His statutes bring us joy. My great-grandfather's story may bring me laughter, but God's Story brings me joy.

Your earthly heritage may bring you pain and sorrow, or happy memories. If there is hurt in your heritage, my heart goes out to you. But whatever your earthly history, remember that God's statutes are your true heritage. Claim victory and joy in that promise. Pray now for healing from any hurt caused by your ancestors. Pray that God will give you joy in your true heritage in His statutes.

OUR RELATIONSHIP WITH HIM

Read Psalm 43:4

As I sit here pondering the enormity of the lessons to be learned in this verse, I am at a loss to put my thoughts into words. The psalmist brought his offerings to a physical altar where animals were sacrificed over fire. In churches the steps onto the stage or the pews set up at the front are sometimes called the altar. Sometimes my altar is in the car driving down the road. Sometimes my altar is my bed as I go to sleep or when I wake up in the middle of the night. I generally think of my altar as the spot on the couch where I usually sit for my morning quiet time. But honestly, some mornings it's just a place where I sit and selfishly focus on other things besides God. Our altar is anywhere our relationship with God grows, where we acknowledge our sin and our dependence on Him, where we seek Him. Our altar is anywhere His Word touches our hearts and changes us. When our hearts are malleable toward Him, He brings us closer to Himself and fills us with joy and delight.

Wherever you are right now, you can go to the altar of God and find joy and delight. Take a moment and go to His altar now.

RELATIONSHIP IS RECOGNIZABLE

IN HIS CREATION

Read Psalm 65:8

My favorite places to worship and have personal time with God are just about anywhere outside. I love spending time with God on a balcony in Galveston overlooking the waves of the gulf pounding the beach, at a campsite at Greers Ferry Lake or Carlyle Lake watching the sunrise, in an atrium looking at the glacier at Lake Louise, on a rock in the beautiful Ozark mountains, or on my own back porch looking at the pasture. God's creation is full of beauty and every sight brings me joy and fills me with awe. I was talking with someone recently who is unsure of their belief in God. He hasn't completely rejected but hasn't fully committed either. One statement he made goes along with this verse, and with Romans 1: 19-20. "When I look at nature, I just don't think all this beauty could have happened randomly." Well said. Nature declares the glory of God and fills us with His joy.

Read Psalm 96:12

Even though I am in the house right now, in my mind I can hear the fields and trees sing for joy. I have heard it so many times. Go outside anywhere in the country near sunset or early in the morning. Listen to the frogs croaking. Listen to the crickets singing. Listen to the coyotes howling. (I don't really like this sound.) Listen to the leaves rustling in the breeze. Listen to the cows mooing and the donkeys braying. Nature sings perpetual songs of joy to God. (Let me add a side note here. I am not what we call a "tree hugger." We must not worship nature itself. God put humans on the earth to manage the creation He made. We are to use it wisely. We are not to worship the created things. We worship only the creator. Please be aware of this distinction and do not fall into the trap of worshiping Mother Nature, Earth Day, and so forth. Worship God only.)

If you are in a location where you can, step outside. Look at God's creation. Listen to the songs of joy being sung by His creation. Join in joyful worship of the God who created all things.

IN HIS PROTECTION

Read Psalm 5:11

A restaurant owner in our small town changed tremendously when he was miraculously saved. When needy people came into his restaurant, he would give them something to eat. He would then call my husband to come talk to them while they ate. One time a man said that he needed to go to a larger city nearest us and asked my husband to drive him to the truck stop so that he could try to get a ride. As they were driving along, my husband made small talk. He asked the man how long he had been on the road. The man said, "Three years. It's hard to get a job when you have been in prison. I killed my mother. I'm not sorry about it either." Probably not the safest person to have in the car with you. But God protects those who take refuge in Him, and there is joy in that assurance.

We had been to an evangelism conference at Lake Louise, Canada. To catch our flight out of Calgary, we had to leave the hotel before the sun came up. The brightness of the moon illuminated the snow-covered tops of the nearby mountains. Both my husband and I were amazed at the beauty and took our eyes off the road. My husband heard me gasp when I looked back at the road and saw that we were in the midst of a herd of large animals. I think they were moose but I don't really know. It happened so quickly. When I try to remember what they looked like, all I can see is Bullwinkle. (for those of you who don't remember Bullwinkle, he was a cartoon moose during my childhood). (Bill Scott) My husband began to swerve and do some pretty stunt-mannish driving maneuvers, but I know that he was not a good enough driver to bring us through that herd of animals unscathed. God was truly our protection.

Sometimes we fail to see and acknowledge God's protection. Think of times that God has protected you from danger.

IN TRYING TIMES

Read Psalm 94:18-19

A few weeks ago, my daughter in law had some pain in her abdomen and went to the emergency room. They diagnosed her with appendicitis and scheduled her to have her appendix removed that afternoon. Two days later they received the pathology report. She did not have appendicitis at all. What they removed was a relatively large carcinoid cancer of the appendix which had spread to surrounding tissue. She and my son have 4 wonderful children. As their grandmother, I can see how precious they are, but I also know that some of them are pretty high maintenance. They need their mother. Her anxiety was pretty high. We talked and texted quite a bit. I have mentioned before what a heart for God she has. I want to share a short statement that she made. (copied and pasted with her permission from a text conversation)

> "Just pray that it hasn't spread any more than they know it has. That's my biggest emotional hurdle. I know God heals and I know He is good and works all for His glory. I want His will over mine and that is so hard to stomach if that means I go home early. But I can't think that - all day long I have no words other than I trust you, Lord."

In her anxiety she trusted God to support her and bring her joy. Maybe the anxiety you have isn't life or death. Anxiety can come from all kinds of things: health issues, financial struggles, job situations, family conflicts, even anxiety that seemingly comes out of nowhere. Whatever the reason that you feel like your foot is slipping, remember that trusting in God to give you comfort and joy in and through those anxious situations is an act of faith that He will honor. Being wholeheartedly committed to Him does not mean that we will live lives free of anxiety. It does mean that He will comfort us through those situations and bring us joy in Him.

Are you experiencing anxiety about a certain situation now? If so, take a moment to realize that by submitting to God and trusting Him, comfort and joy are available to you. Your situations may not change, but God will work in your heart to bring you joy.

IN REPENTANCE

Read Psalm 51:10-12

David's willingness to repent and return to fellowship with God is key to the phrase so often used to describe him. "David was a man after God's own heart." Wouldn't it be wonderful if God said about us, you and me, that we are people after His own heart? Oh, how I long for that to be true, but I know that often I don't acknowledge my sinfulness and repent. This verse speaks to the heart of the attitude we need to have. Only God can create a pure heart within me. Only God can renew a steadfast spirit. Our task is to be repentant and yield to Him. When I look at these three verses, I see a circle of God's work in the life of a repentant believer. We make the commitment to yield to Him, and ask Him to grant us a willing spirit to continue in a lifestyle of submission to Him. He creates a pure heart and a steadfast spirit within us. Our lives are filled with the Holy Spirit and we fellowship in His presence. He gives us joy in the salvation that He provides. We continue to yield and ask Him to continue to give us steadfastness in our commitment to Him. Like David, we will sin. That circle will be broken, not by God, but by us. The simple, yet sometimes difficult, solution to that problem is to come to Him in repentance.

Picture the simple toy top. You spin it between your thumb and index finger and it spins in rapid circles on the table or floor. If it is one with colors on it, there is a mesmerizing whirl of color. (Or more recently a fidget spinner) Then...your friend or sibling sticks their finger in the whirl and the top totters and falls over. Think of the smooth and beautiful path of the top as the circle I described above where yielding produces joy. Think of the ugly hand of unrepented sin causing the joy to crash. You pick that top up again and spin it. The beauty begins again. When we allow God to pick up what sin has crashed in our lives, we can once again experience that joy.

IN THE GOOD AND THE BAD

Read Acts 13:48-52

Every time I read this scripture, it strikes me how much damage a bunch of "God fearing," meddling women can do. I surely don't want to be part of that group. But that is a whole different discussion than where we are focusing now. Verse 52 tells us that the disciples were filled with joy. Indeed, they had a few things to be happy about, but let's focus on joy rather than happiness. They were happy that the Gentiles had accepted the Word of the Lord and believed. We are all happy when someone accepts Jesus as their Savior. But then look at the rest of the situation. The Jewish leaders stirred up persecution against Paul and Barnabas, which resulted in them being expelled from the region. Words with strong connotations are used here. The New Oxford American Dictionary says that persecution involves hostility and ill treatment. Expel means to be forced to leave a place. Envision a movie version of a beaten and bruised outsider being hauled off in the back seat of the "good ole boy" county sheriff's patrol car, lights flashing and sirens blaring, and being pushed out onto a dirty gravel road at the county line, with threats of what will happen if you ever set foot in that county again. (I live in the rural south. I know this isn't a prevalent reality. I have, however, seen those kinds of movies.) The persecution the disciples were experiencing was not like the colloquial saying "Don't let the screen door hit you on your way out." This was serious business. Yet, they had joy.

What persecution do we experience? From where have we been expelled? What shame do we have? What inconveniences do we face? Let those be a source of joy, yes, joy to you. Trade them all now for His joy.

Read Romans 12:11-13

If we are talking about spiritual nutrition, these verses are superfood. (I just looked back at the entire 12th chapter of Romans. To get a clear picture of the context of these verses, you may want to read the whole chapter before you continue this section.) Read verses 11-13 again, letting each phrase touch your heart. If we abide in the instruction in verse 11, have a zealous (full of energy and enthusiasm) (New Oxford Dictionary) faith, a spiritual fervor (intense and passionate feelings) (New Oxford Dictionary), and serve the Lord wholeheartedly, the next two verses come more easily. We cannot have the actions and attitudes of verses 12 and 13 unless we are immersed in verse 11. Shortly after I started my current job, we had a week of professional development activities. In one of those the principal gave us each a sticky note on which we were to write one word that explained what we each had to contribute to the school. Then we each walked up to the large poster board and stuck our sticky note up, stating without explanation what we could do for the children. As others began to share their words, I started to want to crawl under my chair and hide. They used words like "love", "compassion", "kindness". Yep. I was feeling really uncomfortable. But I had written my word. Okay. It's my turn. "Advocate". My principal sort of stared at me like I was from Mars. I sat down, embarrassed. But I was honest. I have a zeal for these children who have no one to stand up for them. The vast majority of parents love their kids. But our educational system is so complicated now that they may not even know where to begin to advocate for their children. Sometimes parents are so overwhelmed with their own concerns that they don't see how their children are struggling. Sometimes they are high or drunk. Sometimes they are having too much fun to care about their children. I won't go on with my rant. You get the point. I have intense and passionate feelings for these children. That's not a bad thing, because I believe with all my heart that God put me where I am for that very purpose. But I have to ask myself the question. Am I as zealous for Him as I am for the ministry He has given me? He can't use me nearly as effectively in the ministry until I am zealous for Him personally. You may feel passionately that God has put you in your job, your family, or some other ministry for His perfect purpose and have great zeal for the purpose He has given you. I pray that you have that assurance.

Ask yourself the question. Do you have as much zeal and fervor for your relationship with Him as you do for the jobs, tasks, and ministries He has given you?

That is the background. Now, let's look at the joy. Joyful in hope. When I think about some of the children and the horrible situations they live in daily, it's difficult to remain hopeful for them. Some of their minds and bodies have been so scarred by the drugs, alcohol, neglect, and abuse that only a miracle will give them hope for their future. I even feel that way about my own life sometimes. Circumstances can be overwhelming. But, when we live in zeal and fervor for our relationship with Christ, He gives us a hope that is beyond our circumstances, a hope that rests fully in Him and Him alone.

Are you living with a hope beyond your circumstances? Does your fervor and zeal for God overshadow any feelings of hopelessness? Commit and yield to Him, asking that He gives you a zeal and fervor for Him that spills out as hope in all circumstances.

CHAPTER 7

RESPONSES TO RELATIONSHIP

IN SACRIFICIAL GIVING

Read 2 Corinthians 8:1-3

So many strong words and phrases in these verses! Very severe trial–Overflowing joy. Extreme poverty– Rich generosity. Let those soak into your mind and heart. Scripture pairs these things that we view as total opposites. I have been to Kisumu, Kenya two times to teach Bible studies, do some construction (that is funny because I am not handy like that, but I did stir up some concrete with a shovel and hand some rocks to the next person in the line) and generally minister to some people who live in extreme poverty. I have never witnessed such poverty in the United States. Never. People were living in huts made from sticks and cow manure, with rags stuffed in the holes where the cow mature had cracked and fallen out. Women carried dirty water in five-gallon containers on their heads to huts without plumbing or electricity. One of the ministries we worked with taught the women to sew so that they could make some money for necessities. Even though several Bibles were available for people to use at the Bible studies, one of the women did not have a Bible. I let her use mine. She was so thrilled to have it that I told her she could keep it. I had others at home, so this was not a sacrifice to me. (The average daily wage there is $1.00 per day. Compare that with the cost of a Bible. Hardly anyone in this group of women could afford to purchase a Bible.) But the day we were to leave, she brought me a gift of a dress she had sewn. This was a huge sacrifice to her. Had I not taken it, she would have been deeply offended. That dress was made with some kind of fabric that makes me itch, plus she must have thought I was much skinnier than I am, but that dress speaks volumes to me about sacrificial giving out of extreme poverty.

Think of examples of overflowing joy in severe trials, and rich generosity out of extreme poverty. Praise God for the experience or the example.

IN UNITY

Read Philippians 2:1-3

Joy that comes from unity is wonderful. But unity is difficult. And the closer the relationships the harder it is to have unity. I know: that didn't make any sense on the surface. Who do you argue with most, your spouse and your children, or your acquaintances? Who can hurt you the worst? One Christmas I was in the kitchen preparing some part of the family meal. My two daughters were sitting at the kitchen table, having a pleasant conversation. I watched as they both exploded in anger toward the other. I was standing right there and still don't understand what happened. They each said extremely hurtful things to each other, things they knew would be painful, because they knew each other well. Unity is difficult in close relationships because we know how to hurt each other. When this disunity exists, it hurts not only the parties involved, but also others around you. That was an isolated event. They generally get along just fine. Both are English majors, love literature, and frequently have pleasant conversations about teaching English to students in their jobs. Whatever precipitated their argument was not typical for them. The same thing can happen within the family of believers. Minor disagreements can escalate. It's painful for everyone. Paul is asking the believers at Philippi to have unity. First, he explains that the foundation of unity rests in the encouragement and comfort God's Spirit gives us. The unity we have is a result of His work in our lives. He gives us tenderness and compassion. Paul then lists a series of attitudes and actions that promote unity. When we allow His Spirit to work in us, we have a love for our brothers and sisters in Christ. We put others above ourselves. We are humble in spirit and action. God's Holy Spirit gives us the characteristics that promote the kind of unity that brings joy to those around us. Paul implored the believers to make his joy complete by having this kind of relationship with God that results in unity among believers.

Think about true humility that is the result of the Spirit's work in your life? Self-evaluate your submission to Him. Is your humility reflected in your relationships in your family, church, and workplace? Pray that He will work in your life to bring true humility, unity and joy in fellowship.

GIVING THANKS TO THE FATHER

Read Ephesians 5:18-20

I've been staring at this scripture for three days now, off and on, waiting to hear what God is teaching me through these words. I think that if the wait is this long, and my heart can't move on to something else, it must be important.

Paul encourages the believers in Ephesus to allow the Spirit to fill their lives, resulting in a lifestyle of encouragement to other believers, praise, joy, and thanksgiving to the Father. When the Spirit reigns in us, He overflows into our conversation. He asks us to speak to one another with songs that come from His Spirit. How often do we say "I have this song in my head and I just can't get it out."? I have bus/cafeteria duty in the mornings. After all the children have eaten their breakfast, one of the teachers leads them in some songs to keep them occupied until it is time to go to class. She sings "Head and shoulders, knees and toes" with them often. I get that song in my head and sing it all day. It's so annoying, but I can't help it. It is in my head. That is a song that we had ingrained in us since early childhood. I realize I am getting slightly off topic, but this is my pet peeve #347. Parents and childcare workers at church should be singing spiritual songs to children from infancy. Just as "Head and Shoulders, Knees and Toes" is deeply implanted in our brains, songs of praise to God should also be in our earliest memories. We need to have psalms, hymns, and spiritual songs so ingrained in our heads that they overflow from our hearts and our mouths.

What songs are stuck in your head? Are these songs ways that we encourage other believers? Are these songs music to God's ears, given with praise in our hearts?

Whatever is in our mind is what comes out of our mouths. That's really scary, isn't it? One of my daughters was like that as a child, and still is to a certain degree as an adult. We used to say that she had no filter between her brain and her mouth. My granddaughter is the same way. A few weeks ago, I stayed at their house while their mother was in the hospital. Her family has a full-size SUV. I have a mid-size SUV. Every day for the entire ride to her school in the morning and back in the afternoon, she told me how much she hated my little car, that her siblings were in her space, and that being in the horrible little car gave her a headache. Bless her heart. God has blessed her daddy with an intellect and personality that has allowed him to minister to others through his job and be successful in the eyes of the world. They live in a large house in an affluent neighborhood. She has godly parents who seek God's will in everything and teach their children the importance of putting God first. Yet, she did not have a thankful heart. (I admit I was pretty frustrated with her and told her that she needed to live in a mud hut in Africa for a while. I know. Bad Nanna.) During the Thanksgiving season a few years ago, I asked one of my students "What are you thankful for?" (yes, I ended that sentence with a preposition) He said, "I'm thankful that my mom has a job cleaning the motel rooms because people throw away perfectly good food that she can bring home to us." That makes me want to cry every time I think about it. This precious child had a thankful heart. God asks us to give thanks in everything as His Spirit overflows in us.

Do you have a thankful heart in all things? Pray that God's Spirit will fill you with thanksgiving in all things.

Read Revelation 4:8-11

I cannot even begin to picture this in my mind. The angels in continual songs of praise to God. The twenty-four elders falling down in praise and thanksgiving to Him. He alone is worthy! I work hard at my job, and sometimes I think it is a thankless job. I start thinking that I deserve some praise for a job well done. Admit it. You do too. But that is so self-centered. Only God is worthy of praise. My mother's favorite song was "Will There Be Any Stars in My Crown" (Eliza E. Hewitt). As I grew older and studied the scriptures more, I began to question the theology in that song. (Pet peeve #678: Just because a song is sung in church doesn't mean that it is theologically correct.) The twenty-four elders do have crowns, but look what they do with them. They lay them down before God on His throne, because only He is worthy. I'm not saying that God won't reward us for our commitment to Him. We receive a crown of glory (Hebrews 2:9), a crown that will last forever (1 Corinthians 9:25) a crown of victory (2 Timothy 2:5), a crown of life (James 1:12). There are scriptures that make that clear. (Matthew 25: 23) And yes, He wants us to acknowledge that He has created us according to His perfect plan. (Genesis 1:27, Psalm 139: 13, Ephesians 2:10) He wants us to be encouraged in the work He has given us to do here. (Acts 9:31, Romans 1: 11-12, Romans 15: 4-5) Any feelings of self-loathing are not from God. But when we are in His Presence, we will not seek any honor for ourselves. All praise and glory belong to Him alone.

Pause a moment to contemplate the honor He deserves.

BENEFITS OF RELATIONSHIP

SHARING IN THE SAINTS' INHERITANCE IN THE LIGHT

Read 1 Peter 1:3-5

Our inheritance begins with the new birth He has given us through the resurrection of Jesus. We have that inheritance from that point on. God's power then protects us spiritually as we await the ultimate culmination of our inheritance, which comes in Heaven when we are in the presence of God for eternity.

I don't have a big imagination. I tend to see things as I have seen things. I have read about the street of gold, the gates of pearl, the river of life but I honestly cannot visualize what heaven will be like. But I have assurance that Heaven is where my inheritance is kept. Christians tend to think that Heaven is the supreme inheritance for which we wait and even long. But look again. This scripture does not say that Heaven is our inheritance. It says that our inheritance is kept in Heaven. What is that inheritance? Being in the presence of God! Heaven is an unimaginable place not only because of the grandeur of its beauty, but more importantly because we will dwell there eternally in the presence of God.

Read Acts 20:32

In Paul's farewell to the believers at Ephesus he gave them encouragement to commit themselves to God based on the word of His grace. His grace toward us forms the solid foundation of salvation upon which our spiritual growth is built. Once that foundation is poured out on us by His grace, His grace builds us up spiritually. Our inheritance among the sanctified is not simply an end, but it is the process of being built up in His grace, which is culminated when we worship in His presence in Heaven. Don't miss the imagery this short verse provides us of what God is doing in us.

Stay with me here. We know that scripture tells us that He pours out His love to us through His Spirit. (Romans 5:4) See the concrete truck pouring the solid foundation. There are 75 references in scripture to foundations: of creation, of Solomon's temple, of the rebuilt temple, of His throne, and of Jesus as our salvation. God takes foundations very seriously. When we accept Jesus' gift of salvation and His Spirit comes to dwell within us, the firm foundation is laid. Upon that foundation we are built up in Him through His ongoing work in us. The project isn't complete until we enter Heaven where the inheritance of being with Him forever awaits us. The theological terms are justification (laying the foundation at our salvation), sanctification (the process of spiritual growth) and glorification (Heaven).

Read Isaiah 33:5-6

Based on this scripture, what are the components of this sure foundation?

I truly apologize if I am carrying this analogy too far, but this is how my brain works. We need cement, sand and/or gravel, and water to mix the concrete. But to make the concrete even more stable, we add rebar before we pour in the mixture. The fear of the Lord is the rebar. It comes first and is the stabilizing factor. The fear of the Lord, a reverence for Who He is, leads to an acceptance of His salvation, which results in our growing in wisdom and knowledge. Zion, the city of God, is filled with His justice and righteousness. In theological terms Zion can refer to many things. I'm not a Biblical scholar, so I may be taking things out of context here, but for the sake of discussion, let's view Zion as the life of the believer, the place where His Spirit dwells. On that foundation, righteousness and justice are being built. God is exalted as others observe this building process in us.

Read Luke 6:47-49

Read 1 Corinthians 3:10-15

A friend loaned me a book several years ago. I don't remember the name of the book or the author. The premise of the book was based on these verses. It was quite thought provoking. I pray that I am not plagiarizing in any way that author's thoughts.

When a house burns, the homeowners often search through the ashes looking for anything they can salvage. When the debris is cleaned away, all that is left is the foundation. It is a nightmare for the homeowners. "We lost everything" is sometimes their emotion. Everything perishable is gone, completely incinerated or ruined beyond use. Only those things that are purified by fire remain. I honestly don't know what that would be in a house fire. I can't imagine being able to find the remains of jewelry in the ashes. I picture things like iron skillets. But we know that God sees all things. He can see even the minutest treasures that survive the fire. It is eye opening to think about what portions of my life will survive this test. This is a concept that I do not understand. My feeble mind does not grasp what kind of reward system Heaven holds for us. However, we do have the comfort that the foundation will remain. That foundation is Jesus. Our salvation is only through Him, and that hope is secure through His work. Our works do not earn us salvation. Our actions do have significance, but for reward, not salvation.

Read Ephesians 2:20-21

Read Ephesians 1:15-21

This passage is so rich in explaining our inheritance that I feel the need to just sit and stare at the words in amazement. I cannot even begin to comprehend the blessing we receive as our inheritance! We can have this inheritance because of Jesus. He was crucified, resurrected and is seated at the right hand of God in heavenly realms. He has all authority, power and dominion. His name is greater than any other name.

By faith we accept this inheritance. The beginning of our inheritance is salvation. The culmination of our inheritance is eternity in the presence of God. Between these two events we also receive wonderful portions of our inheritance. He gives us the Spirit of wisdom and revelation so that we can continually know Him better. He opens the eyes of our hearts, our understanding, so that we can know the hope to which we are called. The same incomparably great power that raised Jesus from the dead works in us. He shows us the richness of the inheritance He has for us. My husband's friend made a statement one time that explains the spiritual inheritance we enjoy here on this earth.

He said, "Even if heaven weren't real, and I believe it is, the joy of having a relationship with Jesus here on earth would be worth accepting Him." We miss out on so much if our commitment to Him is too weak to recognize the blessing (inheritance) we have right now. I want to say so much more about this passage but the words escape me. Let God speak to you personally as you look closely at these scriptures.

Read each phrase of this passage (Ephesians 1: 15-21). Contemplate every blessing at our disposal. Ask for understanding of the enormity of God's power working in us. Meditate on these verses.

RESCUED FROM DARKNESS

Read John 8:12

We are rescued from eternal darkness, hell, separation from God, when we accept Christ Jesus as our Lord and Savior. We will never walk in darkness. Think about that. "Never" is a strong word. Jesus does not say "you won't usually walk in darkness" or "you will walk in light for a while then it will be dark again." Never walk in darkness! When we follow Him, we have the light of life. Period. For eternity.

We live in the country. In the country dark is **dark.** We have a light on our back porch but not in our carport. In the morning when I leave for work, I am carrying my computer bag, my purse, my coffee, and a mug with ice in it for later in the day. Sometimes other stuff, but always those things. As I go down the steps, my shadow blocks the light from the porch. I cannot see the steps. Every morning, I am aware of the need to carefully watch my steps so that I do not fall. Walking in the dark is dangerous. Walking in spiritual darkness has even more dangerous consequences. But in Jesus we always walk in the Light.

Read John 3:18-20

Jesus is the Light that reveals our sinfulness and frees us from the darkness of condemnation. Why then do we avoid coming to Him in faith? Why do we have fear that our sinful deeds will be exposed? One of my students has significant speech- language, learning and behavior issues. He will use just about any tactic to avoid working. In order to go from his Kindergarten classroom to my therapy room, we have to walk out the door and down a covered sidewalk into another building. If the sun is shining, he immediately starts covering his eyes and screaming that the sun hurts his eyes. Interestingly, the sun does not hurt his eyes when he is at recess. It is not the sunshine itself that hurts his eyes; it is the change from his classroom to a more intensive therapy situation. Because he has so many deficits, therapy is something that he needs, yet he avoids it. Aren't we the same way when confronting our sin? Having our sin exposed by His Light can be a painful experience, yet it produces a sorrow that leads to repentance. This little fellow already has speech language deficits. We already have a sinfulness that deserves condemnation. We both need to be exposed to light to address the changes that need to take place in our hearts and our minds.

Salvation versus lostness is the connotation we most often associate with scriptural references to darkness. But when we look closely at scripture, there are other associations. Metaphorically, darkness can mean many things. Sadness. Evil. Sinfulness. Depression. Hell.

Read Exodus 20:18-21

God had just given the Ten Commandments to Moses. The people were terrified. They watched as Moses approached the thick darkness where God was. Why does scripture use these words? "... the thick darkness where God was." I may be pushing the limits of biblical interpretation here, but bear with me. They were on the outside looking in, but not seeing. The darkness obscured God from them. Skip ahead to Exodus 34: 29. Moses's face was radiant when he returned from the mountain. It was not dark where Moses met with God. It only looked dark to the people from the outside. Darkness is what hides God from us. What can that darkness be? All those words we listed earlier. Sin. Evil. Sadness. Depression. And many more things. We are rescued from that darkness by Jesus. But we have to allow Him to work in our lives through the darkness to the point that we can truly see Him.

Read Psalm 107:10-14

I'm not sure of the situation the psalmist was experiencing when he wrote these words. We do know that many of the psalms are messianic prophecies. I believe that some are applicable in more than one way. First, let's look at the messianic prophecy regarding our salvation. We lived in rebellion to God, and were prisoners to our sin. Darkness surrounded us because we were separated from God. We are rescued from darkness when we cry out to God. He saves us and breaks the chains of sin and death.

Thank God for rescuing you from darkness when you accepted Him as Savior.

Some (we) sat in utter darkness. Sitting implies that we are comfortable in our darkness. When I come home from work, I want to sit on my end of the couch and do mindless things. I'm totally unproductive. Even though there are things I could and should be doing when I come home, I choose to sit. We choose to sit in darkness when we rebel against God's commands and despise His plans. When we choose rebellion, we experience consequences. After I have chosen unproductive sitting for an extended period of time, I often look around me at the unaccomplished tasks and go into a rant about living in total filth. When we make the spiritual choice to sit comfortably in unconfessed sin, not only are we unproductive in our walk with God, but filth begins to build up in our lives that further separates us from a wholehearted life. When I realize the physical filth around me, I may go into a cleaning frenzy in an attempt to repair the damage my sitting has caused. Thankfully, God has provided a better way for us when we have allowed darkness to enter our lives. When we cry out to Him, He rescues us.

In what darkness do you choose to sit? Whatever it is, cry out to God to free you.

Read Psalm 143:3-4

The enemies who pursue us take many forms. My daughter in law was recently diagnosed with a rare form of cancer. She told me a few days ago that she is having a difficult time staying out of a dark place. On the surface it seems clear that the enemy is cancer, but the enemies are also pain and fear. She has a strong faith and commitment to God, but she is facing temptation. The pain she feels physically is tempting her to fear that the treatment will not be successful or that she will deal with ongoing pain for years. She understands that God is her strength and her deliverer, but the temptation is still there. Your dark place may be physical illness, financial obligations, family relationships, job stress, or a myriad of other things. You may be drawn to, or forced into that darkness. The only light is through trust in God. The psalmist pours his heart to God, asking God to rescue him.

Identify the enemy that pulls you into darkness. Ask God to defeat that enemy and bring you into light.

TRANSFERRED INTO THE KINGDOM OF THE SON HE LOVES

Read John 3:5-8

There are 119 references in the gospels to the "kingdom". Jesus explained the Kingdom of God using parables and other figurative language. A recurring phrase is "the Kingdom of God is *like…*" Explaining what is indescribable requires equating that concept to an understandable concept. Anyone who works or lives with children does this on a daily basis. When Nicodemus asked how to enter the Kingdom of God, Jesus told him that he must be born again. Nicodemus was thinking literally and asked how that could be possible. When flesh gives birth to flesh, we become living, breathing souls with a propensity to sin. Up to this point we were dealing with concrete concepts.

We are born. We sin. This is where the concepts become more difficult to explain. To become heirs of the Kingdom of God, a miraculous spiritual birth must happen. We are spiritually born into a spiritual kingdom. It is not something our eyes can see or that our minds can understand without the Spirit of God revealing it to us. We are transformed into a spiritual being and transferred into an indescribable spiritual kingdom.

If you have not been reborn into that spiritual kingdom, I pray that you will enter this kingdom right now. Acknowledge your sinful nature. Believe that Jesus is God who took human form and died a sacrificial death to provide forgiveness for you. Accept Jesus' gift of salvation. Commit your heart to follow Him wholeheartedly. Tell someone your joyful news.

If you have been reborn spiritually and are an heir to this kingdom, think for a minute. How would you describe this spiritual kingdom to someone who has only had a fleshly birth?

Read Mark 10:13-15

For decades this has been one of my favorite passages of scripture. I am overwhelmed with the significance of Jesus's emotional response when the disciples tried to send the children away. Jesus was *indignant!* Oh, the enormity of that concept! For many years God blessed me with the opportunity to teach children at church. Now He only allows me to do that at work and has demoted me to teaching adults at church. (No offense intended.) I truly believe that the people who teach children the foundational spiritual concepts need to be biblical scholars and intense in their spiritual growth. Children are trusting and inquisitive. They trust us to answer their constant questions with a knowledgeable truth. We don't have an opportunity to prepare for the specific questions they ask, because who knows what they will think about and when they will think about it. We must be constantly prepared. If we teach them inaccurate information we can lead them astray for a lifetime. Another personal story that is difficult to share, but applicable to this discussion. After my husband's car accident, our son was struggling with lots of emotions and questions. He is also extremely smart, not bright smart, but gifted smart. If you aren't familiar with the difference, bright kids know the answers to the questions. Gifted students are always questioning, wanting to understand on a deeper level. My son asked his Discipleship Training teacher a difficult question. Rather than admit she didn't know, or tell him she would look into it, she told him not to ask any more questions in her class. From that point forward, he has rejected church. One teacher changed his life. Is that the kind of teacher you want to be? I certainly don't want to change a child's life like that.

What does Jesus' statement in verse 15 teach us as adults?

We must come humbly to Him with complete trust and an insatiable desire to know more about Him, asking Him all the questions and knowing that He will absolutely answer with Truth.

Read Luke 9:57-62

Citizenship and service in the Kingdom of God requires a wholehearted commitment, placing Him above everything else. Do we place conditions on our commitment to follow Him? Jesus knows our hearts. I believe that His response in verse 57 is based on a precondition the man had in his heart. He wanted some kind of certainty that he would have a sense of security and be comfortable. Verse 59 shows a man who wanted to attend to family business before he was willing to follow Jesus. He wanted to stay with his family until his parents died and were buried, and their business was completed, making him financially secure. The man in verse 61 valued his family over obedience to God. Jesus explained the unwavering commitment needed to serve God. I do not have an adventurous heart. I have no desire to climb Mt. Everest, skydive, or even snow ski, but when God called my husband to preach, He led us to leave our home for my husband to go to college. I saw this as the greatest adventure of my life, trusting God completely to care for us as we obeyed His call. We had no guarantees of housing, meals, or income, yet we knew this was what God was leading us to do. Over the next few years, my husband completed his Bachelor of Arts, Master of Divinity, and Doctor of Ministry degrees. We lived in 13 towns in 4 states, and pastored 11 churches. While we were living in other states, my mother, my father-in-law, and my father died. I was a long-distance executrix of my aunt's estate. God never failed to provide for us, both financially and with church family. Do I have any regrets that we chose to follow God's call? Absolutely not. We are not fit for His service if we begin to obey and turn back to second guess our commitment to Him.

What is God asking you to leave behind, never looking back, in order to obey Him completely?

Read Romans 14:17-18

Being citizens of God's kingdom here on earth is a matter of attitude that results from the work of His Holy Spirit within us. We are not so much concerned with eating and drinking, earthly comforts, as with pleasing God. We have peace, joy, and righteousness that pleases God, and is noticed by those around us. I have been watching a miniseries about the history of the British royal family. Elaborate banquets served to dignitaries give the impression of peace, but when the participants go home to their private quarters, they face personal struggles, family disharmony, and uncertainty about how to best address political issues. They live under constant scrutiny by the press and a fear that the facade will fall and their fallacies will be revealed. God's kingdom is very different. His focus is not on food and drink, presenting a facade of peace and righteousness.

Through His Spirit we have real peace resulting in, not only a life pleasing to God, but also a difference in us that is visible and pleasing to our fellow earth-dwellers.

What concerns you most, the daily matters of eating and drinking, your own personal facade, or the attitude of your heart? Do you have peace, joy, and righteousness that comes from yielding to His Spirit's work in your life?

Read 1 Corinthians 4:20

For thirty-five years, my mother worked for a very powerful and influential man. I knew that he had respect for her and trusted her completely to attend to his business. Apparently, this was also common knowledge in his sphere of influence. Even though she kept him informed of the actions she had taken, I knew that a phone call from her was as effective in changing things as a call from him. I knew that he would sign a letter she had written with no questions asked. But to me, he was just a kind man who meant a lot to my mother and to our family. I didn't grasp the significance of any of these things until after my mother had been dead for several years. Someone I know was reminiscing about my mother and said, "She was probably the most powerful woman in our state at that time." Why didn't I know this when I was growing up? Because she didn't talk about it. Not to me. Not to anyone. She didn't have a prestigious title. She was simply a servant empowered to do the work of her employer. When we are servants in the kingdom of God, we are empowered by Him to do His work here on earth. The power isn't our own, and we don't serve Him for our own glory.

Are you quietly and humbly serving with His power, or are you simply talking the talk?

Read Hebrews 12:28

We receive a kingdom that cannot be shaken. Nations rise and fall. Monarchies, dictatorships, republics, democracies, theocracies all are susceptible to peaceful or violent changes in leadership, defeat by enemies, or self-destruction. We, however, are citizens of an everlasting, perfect kingdom built on the solid foundation of Jesus, the solid rock, the cornerstone. This kingdom is ruled with absolute power and wisdom by our loving Savior. Because of this assurance, we are free to give reverent, thankful, awestruck worship to the King of Kings.

Read Revelation 1:5-7

Don't miss the rich content of these few verses. Jesus is ruler of the kings of the earth. Because I watched the miniseries about the British monarchy recently, articles about them pop up in my social media feed. (This in and of itself is slightly frightening, but I digress.) One article mentioned ways those around them must show deference. Even their own family members bow or curtsy. The queen's husband must walk behind her. No one turns their back to her. Jesus is ruler over the kings of the earth. Kings, queens, presidents, prime ministers, dictators, chiefs are all subject to Him. And we are His kingdom and His priests. Why and how did He do this? He loves us. Sounds so simple, yet so overwhelming profound. The Ruler of the kings of the earth loves us. He freed us from our sins by His blood. The Ruler of the kings of the earth died on the cross for you and for me. We have the privilege and the blessing of being servant priests in His kingdom. Again, remember that we become kingdom citizens when we accept Christ as our Savior so even as residents of earth, we are priests commissioned to serve Him. Our service on earth is to reflect His glory. This concept goes back to our original premise. If we are not wholehearted servants, then His glory is not accurately reflected. *Pause to reflect a moment.* Imagine for a moment that our service here is a dress rehearsal for the time we will serve and worship in heaven. There are numerous songs and hymns that mention that we will have a mansion in heaven. Scripture does mention that we will have a home in heaven, and some translations use the word "mansion." However, I have been told that the Greek word translated "mansion" is better translated as "dwelling". That doesn't bother me at all. I don't feel worthy to have a mansion in heaven, and I assume that you don't either. But I do want to serve Him faithfully both here on earth and in heaven for eternity.

Are you, are we, faithfully and humbly serving Him and reflecting His glory to those around us?

He is coming again. Notice that there will be mourning. I heard this story. Someone who denied the existence of God was asked how he would feel if he were wrong. "What will you do if you are wrong? There is a God; you die and are doomed for an eternity in hell?" His flippant response was "Oops." That is absolutely heartbreaking. I feel the physical pain in my heart when I think about this. There will be mourning when unrepentant sinners understand the consequences of their rejection of the loving sacrifice made for them by the Ruler of kings. We, however, will rejoice and praise Him for eternity.

REDEEMED

How does the dictionary define "redeem"? (New Oxford Dictionary)

Redeem (verb) *[with obj.]* 1 compensate for the faults or bad aspects of (something):
2 gain or regain possession of (something) in exchange for payment:

The Levitical Law gave provisions for redeeming property, animals, and even people. When redemption was made, it was because the recipient of the redemption was powerless to redeem themselves. God redeemed the Israelites from slavery in Egypt when they were powerless to redeem themselves. This redemption was a loving act of grace and mercy.

Read Deuteronomy 7:7-9

The theology of God's redemptive plan is mind boggling, and too complex and lofty for my finite mind. But let's just touch on this briefly. These verses remind us that God rescued the people of Israel from their slavery in Egypt because He loved them and because of the oath that He swore to their ancestors, specifically Abraham, Isaac, and Jacob. The promise to Abraham and his descendants was a continuation of the promise he made to Adam and Eve in the Garden. He pronounced His discipline on them for their disobedience in succumbing to the serpent's tempting lies. But in the midst of His discipline, He also promised that the woman's seed would crush Satan. He promised this because He loved Adam and Eve, even in their disobedience. His plan was in place from the beginning. He would redeem mankind from our slavery to sin because He loves us. He promised us that and foreshadowed that in every scripture since the book of Genesis. This covenant of love continues from generation to generation. The entire Old Testament is indeed a testimony and chronicling of His consistency in rescuing His people so that promise would be fulfilled in Jesus.

Read those verses (Deuteronomy 7: 7-9) again and contemplate the enormity of God's promise of love to us.

Read Leviticus 25:47-49

We are redeemed at a great cost. Only the precious blood of Christ could pay the price for our redemption. In the Levitical law, a person who sold themselves into slavery could only be redeemed by a blood relative, or by themselves. Scripture makes it clear, and we even know within our own hearts, that we are powerless to redeem ourselves from our slavery to sin. Therefore, we need a kinsman redeemer to save us. We also know that none of our earthly relatives are worthy to redeem us. God prepared the way for us to understand that Jesus is our kinsman Redeemer by setting into place earthly laws that correlate to His perfect plan of redemption. God Himself in human form paid the price for our redemption by His own precious blood.

Read 1 Peter 1:17-19

A former co-worker was visiting a friend in an apartment complex. Her young son asked if he could play outside. She warned him to stay away from the pool because he didn't know how to swim, but he was curious. She looked out the window to see him struggling for his life in the deep water. Even though she could not swim, she ran out the door, jumped into the pool, and pushed him toward the side of the pool. He grabbed the wall and was saved. She was not. She gave her life for her son because she loved him. I cannot even begin to imagine how her child views this event. I am positive he must feel some guilt since his disobedience led to her death. He must also feel a deep sense of gratitude for what she did for him. We were drowning in our sin and disobedience, but Jesus rescued us. He redeemed us with suffering and humiliation through His precious blood. But He is God. He resurrected from the dead and has an ongoing relationship with us. We were guilty but have been redeemed. We should live with grateful, reverent awe.

FORGIVEN OF OUR SIN

Read Acts 10:43

Several key words and phrases stand out in this short verse. <u>All</u> the prophets testify about Him. From before creation, God had His perfect plan in place to provide forgiveness for our sin. Every word of scripture points to that plan. Why do we study God's Word? Because scripture, every part of it, testifies to us the loving, perfect way by which He provides forgiveness for us. When I was a child, my daddy read or told me stories from the Bible every night before I went to sleep. I am forever grateful that God provided me with a daddy who placed such importance on teaching me scripture. He was a masterful teacher of scripture, and I hung on every word. I don't remember this, but after I was an adult, he told me that I would cry when he told me about the hardships and trials biblical characters faced. Why was my childish heart so touched by these accounts? Because the stories in the Bible are not just stories. They are testimony of His plan. (I have come to be uncomfortable with the terms "Bible Stories" and "Bible Characters" because I think we should have words with a more powerful connotation to describe God's plan being revealed through the lives of these people. Unfortunately, I do not know what those words would be, so I continue to use those inadequate words.) I am writing this paragraph on December 23, so the last few weeks at school have been filled with children's excitement about Christmas. Since I work with children in small groups or individually, they have more opportunity to share their thoughts and ideas with me than they might in a larger group. One child told me that she wanted to remember the true meaning of Christmas. I asked her to explain what she meant. I will try to be as accurate in quoting her as possible. "Jesus came out of Mary and Joseph. They put Him in the hay, but Joseph said 'this won't work. He needs something softer because the hay is pokey'." When I asked where she learned that, she told me "At church." I certainly am not opposed to presenting scripture in interesting and compelling ways, but even with, no, especially with children, we must maintain accuracy of scripture because God gave us His Word with magnificent purpose. <u>All</u> the prophets testify...

Do you have favorite scripture passages (stories), either from your childhood or as an adult? Think about those and consider how God revealed His plan through them.

While I had always loved the narratives of the Bible, I used to think that the books of prophecy were boring and not really applicable to me personally. As I mentioned earlier, God led me to the books of prophecy when our daughter left college without our knowledge to live in the streets and experience things she had not known in her sheltered life. It's sad that it took such a painful situation to turn me to the words of God that so clearly proclaim His plan of salvation and forgiveness. I can now say that the books of the prophets are some of my favorites. When I am reading through the Bible, I look forward to the time when I get to those books, because they are so rich with God's love and His plan.

Pray that God will continue to reveal His truths to you through every word of scripture.

The next key phrase is "to everyone who believes." My mother-in-law belongs to a group who believe that God looks down the tunnel of time and randomly picks people to be forgiven or not forgiven, and that those people who are chosen to have forgiveness do not need to repent and turn from their sin. Those people destined for unforgiveness have no opportunity to repent. We went to a family member's funeral several years ago, and the words of the preacher still haunt me. Even though this man had never repented of his sin, which included drunkenness and abuse of his wife, the preacher said that he was in heaven because he had been elected for forgiveness. Then the most heartbreaking statement, "He didn't know that he was elected, but I know he was." Even more heartbreaking to me is the realization that his wife and children are true believers and knew that their husband and father had never repented. Forgiveness is provided to <u>everyone who *believes.*</u>

The last key phrase in this verse is "through His name." Parents now have books with 40,000 baby names. They search the internet for unique names. Some parents look for names that sound pretty, while others seek names with significance. Our choices of names for our children speak to the process of spiritual growth in our lives. The oldest is named after me and a name that I liked because it sounded nice. The second was named with my maiden name, and his daddy and my grandpa who both had the same name. The third was named based on scripture and the meaning to us was "a witnessing deacon after God's own heart." The fourth meant "princess of God who is faithful". The fifth's meaning to us was "wholehearted warrior who sought after God." But when we talk about the name of God, the name of Jesus, we are talking about the whole of who He is. The great I AM. We receive forgiveness not simply by the use of a word, but by believing in the entirety of God. We believe in faith and accept the gift provided by an indescribable God. Faith in all that His Name communicates is the only way to salvation.

Read Acts 26:17-18

As Paul was speaking to King Agrippa, he explained the commission God had given him to carry the message of salvation to both the Jews and the Gentiles. He was specific as to what that required him to do. God sent Paul to open their eyes. Opening your eyes can be literal, like what we do when we wake up in the mornings. We have been generally oblivious to what happens around us while we sleep. We awaken to face a new day. Building on that concept, the phrase has a deeper meaning when applied to becoming aware of a given situation and facing the reality of that situation. Paul was sent to open our eyes (and of multitudes of other people) to our sinfulness and need for salvation. Once we acknowledge our dark, sinful nature through the conviction of His Spirit, we can turn toward Jesus, the Light of the world. He, and only He, can rescue us from the power of Satan. Through faith in Him we are forgiven and sanctified.

Read Psalm 32:1-2

I know this is wrong, but I admit that it is easier for me to overlook the transgressions of some of my students. One little child in particular comes to mind. He is so excited about life and so eager to please. When I go get students for therapy, I pick a number between one and ten. The child who gets closest gets to be line leader. When this child gets to be leader, he beams with joy. If he doesn't, his little face betrays utter disappointment for about 3 seconds, then he perks up and asks if he can be the door holder. Then he is so excited to be the door holder. He is an excellent line leader. He is just as good at holding the door. If he does anything wrong, which he seldom does, his eyes fill with tears, even if I very gently remind him of my expectations. Why is he so easy to forgive? Why is it easy to overlook his transgressions? The attitude of his heart. (Well, that big smile, red hair and expressive brown eyes don't hurt either.) God sees our hearts and minds. Look at the last phrase in these verses. "...in whose spirit is no deceit." When we acknowledge our sinfulness, have truly repentant hearts, and seek to serve God faithfully, by His grace He forgives our transgressions and covers our sin with the cleansing blood of Jesus. Our sins no longer count against us, and we are truly blessed.

Read Ephesians 1:6-8

I realize we have looked at this verse earlier. Read this verse again slowly, looking at each word, each phrase. Consider what these verses say.

Glorious grace. Freely given. Riches of God's grace. Lavished. All wisdom and understanding. Today just happens to be Christmas Eve. As I sit here in the living room, I see presents under the tree. I love my children and grandchildren and want to give them the best that I can. Within the confines of my finances, I tried to buy them things that they would enjoy or that would benefit them in some way. When you have teens and preteens, that is very difficult. Now think about how God gives to us. He knows everything about us. He knows exactly what we need and what will serve to grow us closer to Him. He is not limited by finances. He gives to us lavishly. I cannot get over that word. Lavished on us!

- verb *[with obj.]* (**lavish something on**) bestow something in generous or extravagant quantities upon (New Oxford Dictionary)

We find it hard to forgive sometimes. I think that is because of how deeply we are hurt by the things that others do or say. My maternal grandmother died when my mother was born. After her mother died, my mother and grandfather lived with my great-grandparents. All of her life, my mother called her grandmother "mama". Her early childhood was happy. She was content. She attended a small one room country school. One day the teacher didn't show up to teach the class. My mother was curious as to where she was. The other children laughed at her because she was apparently the only one who didn't know that her daddy and her teacher were just married and honeymooning. I don't know why my grandfather didn't tell her. I don't think she ever understood that. She was embarrassed and deeply hurt. However, as I remember things, she was very close to her daddy and her step-mother. My grandmother made no distinction between her "real" grandchildren and me. She treated my mother the same way she treated her "own" children. My mother was by her side when she died of cancer. Yet, my mother harbored a sliver of unforgiveness for something that happened when she was twelve years old. God is deeply hurt by our sin. He not only knows our visible sins, He knows the attitudes of our hearts and our thoughts, yet he lavishes forgiveness on us and chooses to forget our sin. Unlike my mother, He is able to completely forgive. He generously and extravagantly bestows redemptive forgiveness on us according to His rich store of grace, and through His own precious blood.

Do you harbor any unforgiveness? Put that into perspective with the lavish forgiveness God gives to us.

When we juxtapose God's forgiveness for us with our forgiveness of others, we cannot help but be convicted. Jesus told several parables of the one who was forgiven most failing to forgive in the smallest things. We must not, and cannot, accept God's forgiveness without forgiving others in the same way that He forgives us.

Read Jeremiah 31:34

Honestly, there are often times when I can't remember where I put my keys, or what I had for lunch. But I remember to hide my wallet every night because I remember the time a few months ago when our son took my credit card without permission, and spent a significant amount of money on a two-week road trip. Since I seldom use that card, I didn't notice the card was missing to check the statement until after he was a thousand miles away. I love him with all my heart, but am deeply hurt that he could do that. I can forgive (mostly.) But I can't forget, because I am paying that bill monthly, and I find it very difficult to trust. Now think about what God tells us in this verse. He will remember our sins no more. What if God remembered every sin we have? He possesses a capacity to purposely forget that we do not have. He literally forgets our sin when we come to Him in repentance and confession. When we know Him, he forgets our past sin.

Read 1 John 2:12

Our sins are forgiven because of His Name. His Name signifies His compassionate mercy and His authority to forgive. We have all known people who were "name droppers." One of my husband's friends in college spoke of well-known pastor personalities using their first names, implying that he was close friends with them. My friend's son-in-law is an attorney. When she was called for jury duty, the judge asked if anyone had any reason they couldn't serve on the jury. My friend raised her hand. When the judge asked her why, she told him the attorney for one of the parties involved was her son-in-law. That's some pretty effective name dropping. Needless to say, she didn't serve on that jury. While some people have names that influence others, no other name compares with His Name. Simply by calling on His name, our sins are forgiven.

> As I have been writing this, I have tried to be open to what God is teaching me in the small things. At times, it seems like there is no end to the information to be shared about this topic and that the process will never end. As I have become impatient that it is taking so long to "finish" this study, I was complaining to God that it is taking forever. In the midst of that prayer, I was reminded that Abraham never saw the complete fulfillment of the promise. Numerous people are mentioned in Hebrews 11 who lived by faith without seeing the promises fulfilled. Another lesson to be learned from my impatience is that living a wholehearted life is indeed a song that never ends. Not all spiritual lessons have to be a theological exposition. Sometimes the simple things are the most applicable.

CHAPTER 8

WHO IS JESUS

Refer back to Colossians 1: 6 which says, "since the day you heard it and recognized God's grace in the Truth." What are we recognizing? We are recognizing WHO Christ is.

When we try to describe Who Jesus Is, we are basically in way over our heads. He is indescribable. But scripture gives us some glimpses.

Read the following verses slowly and think about what they tell us about Jesus. List or underline what they tell us about what Jesus does. He is...Underline or list what you see of who Christ is.

Colossians 1:15-20 New International Version (NIV) 15 The Son is the image of the invisible God, the firstborn over all creation. 16 For in him all things were created: things in heaven and on earth, visible and invisible, whether thrones or powers or rulers or authorities; all things have been created through him and for him. 17 He is before all things, and in him all things hold together. 18 And he is the head of the body, the church; he is the beginning and the firstborn from among the dead, so that in everything he might have the supremacy.19 For God was pleased to have all his fullness dwell in him, 20 and through him to reconcile to himself all things, whether things on earth or things in heaven, by making peace through his blood, shed on the cross.

THE IMAGE OF THE INVISIBLE GOD

Read Hebrews 1:3

We look in the mirror and assume that is an exact representation of how we look. But have you ever tried to look in your ear or the top of your head using a mirror and a hand mirror. I have. I suppose you want an explanation of why in the world I would do that. Yeah. I'm pretty weird. The point is, it is very difficult to do, because the mirror reflects but not perfectly, not in the right direction, not in perspective. I have heard and read lots of mothers use the term "mini me" to refer to their children. I have even told my daughter-in-law that our oldest granddaughter looks just like her. She does show a strong resemblance to her, but she is not an exact representation of her being. She is an individual, showing common traits of both of her parents, some from generations past, some we don't know where she got. My friend Annie had identical twin boys last Spring. Annie works at a different school now, so I only see her through social media, but I can tell you that those identical twin boys are not exact representations of each other. The only exact representation of anything or anyone is Christ and God, because they are one. Jesus is the glory of God, because He is God.

THE FIRSTBORN OVER ALL CREATION

Read Romans 8:28-30

It was God's plan from the beginning that Jesus would be the firstborn of many brothers and sisters. He knew before time began who would choose to accept Him and be justified by His blood. Those who believe become part of God's family. I saw a picture of a newborn on social media last week. The grandmother had commented, "He looks just like his big brother." How many second and subsequent siblings are compared to the firstborn in the family? I would guess that would be a high percentage. Families compare appearance, personality, and achievement. But Jesus is a far superior first-born Son. God purposed that we, as sinners justified and adopted into His kingdom would be like the Firstborn Son, our Savior and Justifier. This passage of scripture is sometimes taken out of context and used for purposes other than what the context suggests. I have heard people say "All things work together for good," implying that everything that happens is good. Our world is populated with sinful men who commit evil acts out of evil hearts. Not everything is good. Look at verse 28 again. God works in all the events in our lives to conform us to the likeness of the Firstborn. Every event that happens in our lives is to make us more like Jesus, which is God's definition of "for our good". We are confused when we misinterpret this to mean a prosperity gospel or a Pollyanna version of life. The message is that we are being conformed to His likeness, His image, becoming like Him. The process of becoming like the perfect firstborn can be painful at times, and often happens as a result of adversity in our lives, yet the result is that we become more like Jesus. This is what it means to live a wholehearted life in Him.

THE CREATOR OF EVERYTHING

Read Revelation 4:11

We accept scripture as God's Word, truth without any error. This verse clearly tells that God created all things by His will, and that creation continues to have its being based on the will of God. My seminary educated husband tells me that the Hebrew word used in Genesis means to create out of nothing. When my son was a teenager, he constantly had an entourage. Most days I cooked for at least four extra teenage boys in addition to our family. At the time, I bought wheat and ground our own flour. I have a family recipe for the best cinnamon rolls ever (obviously my opinion and not fact.) One day I ground wheat, made bread dough, rolled out the dough, covered it in cinnamon and sugar, and baked homemade cinnamon rolls. My son's friend ate several of them, then said, "These are really good, but my mother makes hers from scratch." That statement still puzzles me. (I started to say it makes me scratch my head, but no pun was intended, so I changed that sentence.) Maybe she also grew her own wheat. I did purchase my grain from the food co-op. I thought I had put a lot of effort into the cinnamon rolls and deserved for the young man to acknowledge that I had also made the rolls from scratch. But I most certainly did not create them out of nothing, and was not worthy of glory and honor and praise. Only God creates from nothing. Only God sustains our existence. Only God is worthy.

BEFORE ALL THINGS

Read 2 Timothy 1:9

The concepts of infinity, past and future, are impossible for me to grasp. Just as time goes on into the future, time goes backward without end. God has always been. Some very creative people have given some illustrations of eternity, when speaking of the future. What is even more mind boggling is that eternity goes back in time as well. I have never heard those creative illustrations of eternity past, perhaps because that concept is even more inexplicable than eternity future. My husband uses the phrase, "God is not bound by time and space." Look at 2 Timothy 1: 9 again. God's purpose and grace for our salvation was in place before the beginning of time as we know it. Not only IS Jesus God in a dimension of time beyond our understanding, He showed us grace and purposed to provide salvation for us through His sacrificial death and resurrection even before time existed. Ponder that for a minute.

THE HEAD OF THE BODY, THE CHURCH

Read Ephesians 1:22-23

Almost any organization, business, or government has an organizational chart. A box at the top followed by a series of smaller boxes, with lines drawn to show who is responsible to whom. I'm sure most of you have seen those in your workplaces. Jesus is at the top of the organizational flow chart for, as Buzz Lightyear said in Toy Story (John Lasseter) "Infinity and Beyond." There is no limit to Jesus' power and authority. Our concept of the universe is limited, but His is not. This scripture specifically addresses the organization of the church. Our churches today often are run like businesses. I have even heard the term "Board of Deacons". We will not go into the original purpose for deacons, but the meaning of the word "deacon" is "servant". The pastor is sometimes called the chief executive officer of the church. We have committees for everything. It's ridiculous. We are so concerned about making our organization run smoothly, that we lose sight of the fact that Jesus is the head of the church. For our local churches to function as we are intended to function, we must acknowledge Who Jesus Is. When we as individuals are wholeheartedly committed to following Him, the local church will be efficient, effective, and powerful. There is no other way.

THE BEGINNING

Read John 1:1-3

The Word is Jesus. He was in the beginning with God, because He IS God. He made all things. As previously stated, I am not a Biblical scholar, but I have been told that the word translated "Word" in these verses is the Greek word "logos", from which we derive our word "logic". When we discuss personality types, we generally make a distinction between those who are creative and those who are analytical/logical. We talk about the left brain and right brain. God is neither right brained nor left brained. He is both logical and creative. Take that thought another step. It is logical that He is the Creator of all things.

THE FIRSTBORN FROM THE DEAD

Read Revelation 1:5-6

While there are references in scripture to others who were resuscitated from the dead, Jesus is the first to be resurrected. But He will not be the last. We will all be resurrected. Even here on earth, we live a resurrected life. We are reborn from the death of sin and resurrected to live as citizens of God's Kingdom. God's love for us was the motivation for His sacrificial death. Death had no power over Him. By His own power, He became the firstborn from the dead so that we could be His Kingdom, and priests to serve Him, giving Him glory in all things.

FIRST PLACE IN EVERYTHING

Read John 3:31-35

John the Baptist testifies to Jesus' identity in the preceding verses. Even though John had possibly known Jesus when they were children, (see Luke 1) through the Holy Spirit's revelation John understood who Jesus IS. Jesus has everything in His hands. John's explanation of who Jesus Is, and how he was able to grasp this, also applies to our relationship with Jesus. He came into the world from His place in Heaven. Many did not then, and do not now, accept His testimony, but to those who do accept Him, He gives His Spirit without limit. We limit Him by our failure to accept and yield to Him. Acknowledgement of His rightful possession of all things is key to developing a wholehearted relationship with Him.

Read Ephesians 1:21

I recently watched a drama on television in which representatives of three different countries were claiming jurisdiction to investigate a crime. There was a lot of bluffing, and huffing and puffing in their efforts to claim authority. There was name dropping, calls to various people whose names and positions represented power. We have no reason for concern. Our Lord has jurisdiction over the entire universe. He did in the past. He does in the present. He will in the future. Forever. Always. The characters in this drama were totally committed to carry out their duties in the service of their country and their authorities. How much more should we have a wholehearted commitment to the One who is above all.

THE FULLNESS OF GOD

Read Colossians 2:9-12

Look carefully at Colossians 2: 9-12. Underline the prepositional phrases. Highlight the verbs. Circle the adjectives. Look specifically at the ones that tell us who Jesus is, what He has done for us, and how He accomplishes His work in us. Meditate on what you see.

Understanding who Jesus is has significance because we cannot, and should not, be wholeheartedly committed to someone we do not know personally. We come to know Him personally when we accept Him as Savior. We learn more about Him through His indwelling Spirit's teaching as we study His Word, pray, and fellowship with other believers.

He is all the fullness of the Deity in bodily form. Is. All. Fullness. Deity. In Sunday School lessons and sermons, you have heard "He was 100% man and 100% God." We accept that by faith. I am captivated by this word "fullness" yet am having trouble grasping exactly what this means. Look at the dictionary definition. "Fullness—filled to capacity, being complete or whole, all that is contained." (New Oxford Dictionary) He is **completely** filled to capacity with all that is contained in the Deity. This fullness of the Deity lives in Him. Notice that this scripture uses the present tense verb. Not "lived." "Lives." He walked this earth in human form, was crucified, buried, and <u>resurrected</u>. Because He is the fullness of the Deity, He is the head over every power and authority. If you are a student of history or keep up with current events, you realize that there have always been and continue to be rulers and governmental authorities who are full of themselves, egotistical and power hungry. They talk big. Jesus has complete power and authority over them. They are absolutely nothing in comparison to Him.

When we realize who He is, we can begin to understand what He has done for us. He <u>brings us to fullness</u>. Referring back to the definition in the previous paragraph, He brings us to a state of being filled to capacity, being complete or whole, and having all that is contained in a personal relationship with the One who is the fullness of God and head over all power and authority. Think about that. Why would we not want that? The resulting benefits of a wholehearted commitment to Him are mind boggling. He circumcised us with a spiritual circumcision. In western cultures physical circumcision is done primarily for health benefits. In Jewish culture circumcision was also a symbol of being set aside to God, a special people. Spiritual circumcision sets us apart as God's children, His people, His kingdom because our old sinful self is cut off. We experience spiritual health benefits as freedom from the sin that enslaved us.

He produces benefits in us by His Deity, His fullness, His power and authority when we accept Him by faith. The loving grace of God purposed that He would die a sacrificial death on the cross and be buried. The powerful work of God resurrected Him. Baptism is a representation of His work in us. By faith in Him, we die to sin and are resurrected to fullness in Him.

RECONCILING EVERYTHING TO HIMSELF

Read Romans 5:10-11

I don't think I have any enemies. I'm sure there are plenty of people who don't like me, and those who I don't like very much either, but I honestly don't categorize any of these people as enemies. That is such a strong word. But we were God's enemies. Sometimes the word order doesn't make any difference. Sometimes it makes a huge difference. "We were God's enemies" or "God was our enemy." Think about it. Those two sentences do NOT mean the same thing, do they? Would you sacrifice yourself or your child for someone you considered an enemy? I have honestly asked myself if I would even be willing to sacrifice myself for my husband, children, or grandchildren. I would hope that I would, but I just do not know. I don't think we ever know until we are placed in that situation. Now, think about this. God, in human form, sacrificed Himself for us when we were His enemies! In human terms, that is incomprehensible.

My parent's best friends' grandson was killed in an all-terrain vehicle accident when he was just a teenager. His organs were donated to several recipients. I know that his parents felt a connection to people they did not even know because their son lived in them. They didn't purposely sacrifice their son, but because of his death, other lives were saved or given a better quality of life. Now, through Jesus' death, He lives in us. What these verses tell us makes perfect sense, even from our human viewpoint. If God sacrificed His Son to reconcile us, how much more will our lives be blessed and enriched and empowered when He lives in us. His sacrificial death brought us salvation, but His resurrected Life brings us a reconciled life in Him. And we boast in Him for what He has done for us. My best friend's grandson was born with heart defects and needed a heart transplant as soon as possible. He lived almost 2 months with outside sources keeping him alive. Then another family lost their baby. My friend's grandbaby received that baby's heart. Every year on the anniversary of his heart transplant, my friend's daughter and son in law post a thank you letter to the parents of the baby who gave their baby life. They don't know who they are, but they constantly remember their sacrifice and their gift. Should we not also boast in Jesus for what He did and does for us?

Are you boasting in Jesus (praising Him) for reconciling you to Himself, even when you were His enemy? Are you boasting about Him for what He does for you, in you, and through you daily? Take some time to think about that from the perspective of my parent's friends and my friends.

Read 2 Corinthians 5:17-20

Our reconciliation to God changes us. We become a new creation. We are different. For some of us, this change is something we know in our own hearts and outward visible changes emerge slowly as we grow closer to God. For others, our friends and family see sudden, if subtle changes. For others the observable change is nothing short of amazing. Louis was a bookie, had an illegal gambling operation in an outbuilding by his house, and was a heavy drinker. A friend of his asked him to listen to his testimony on the local radio station. Louis listened for a few minutes, turned off the radio and started drinking. A few hours later, he called his friend, and told him, "Get your preacher and whoever else you can get to come with you and come out here. I can't take this!" My husband and a few other men from church went to his house. He accepted Christ as his Savior.

The next day he took all of his gambling equipment, all his alcohol, and the book that showed what the gamblers owed him, out into the yard and set it all on fire. Those in the know said there were hundreds of thousands of dollars-worth of gambling debts (maybe more) burned in that fire. From that moment forward he was miraculously changed. He became a close friend to us and was like another grandpa to our daughter. He was truly a new creature. God is <u>who</u> makes us new. We cannot reform ourselves into a new creation. We can slightly improve our behavior, but we are still the old sinful creature. As I have mentioned before, we have tried multiple "healthy" diets to improve our health. For over 3 years, I faithfully adhered to a low carbohydrate diet. Then just one little lapse for a special occasion. Do you think that worked out? No. I went into a carbohydrate downward spiral. Under my own power, I could change my behavior with some success, but I am still a carbohydrate loving being. Only through salvation and yielding to Him are we truly new creatures.

With our reconciliation comes a commission as ambassadors to the world around us, sharing the good news with others. An ambassador is a person who acts as a representative. We are representatives of Christ in the world for the purpose of sharing the reconciliation that is available to all who will come to Him. Lonnie had a gambling addiction. He was hundreds of thousands of dollars in debt. Because of his gambling, his marriage was falling apart. One day he realized that he desperately needed something or someone who could change him. Driving down the road, he noticed a bumper sticker on the car in front of him that said, "Jesus Saves." He didn't know these people, but he followed them to their house and asked them what that meant. He accepted Christ as his Savior. From that moment forward, he became an outspoken ambassador for Christ. His marriage was restored. We had the privilege of knowing him and his family as dear friends. Everywhere he went, he told people about what Jesus had done for him. He was the one who asked Louis (see above) to listen to his testimony on the radio and introduced him to Christ.

When God reconciles us to Himself, He uses the new creature we have become to share His message of reconciliation and bring others to Himself.

MAKING PEACE THROUGH THE BLOOD ON HIS CROSS

Read John 16:33

The peace we experience through Jesus' blood can be a confusing topic. Jesus explained to the disciples that the world would hate them because the world hated Him. (Matthew 10: 22, Matthew 24: 29, John 15: 18). He also told them that He did not come to bring peace to the earth (Matthew

10: 34-36, Luke 12: 51). Yet, He repeatedly used the phrases "Go in Peace," "My peace I give you," "Peace be with you." His Name is Prince of Peace (Isaiah 9:6). In this passage He tells the disciples that in Him they can have peace, and immediately follows with the statement that in this world they will have trouble. So how do we reconcile these seemingly conflicting concepts? His peace is a peace within our hearts unaffected by outward circumstances. If we expect our earthly lives to be a "bed of roses" we will be disappointed. The peace we experience was purchased by His blood. The Rose of Sharon (Song of Solomon 2:1) wore a crown of thorns. In my yard I have a Rose bush and a Rose of Sharon bush. The rose bush has thorns. There are no thorns on the Rose of Sharon. As you have gathered, I like to think that God has a lesson to teach us in even the most mundane and common things in life. I stretch the point sometimes, but bear with me here. When we are IN the Rose of Sharon, we are not among the thorns. The phrase "a bed of roses" has come to mean a carefree and comfortable life. But those roses are surrounded by thorns. Someone has to suffer the thorns for anyone to have a bed of roses. Jesus endured not only the thorns, but also the flogging, the scourging, the nails, the cross, the sword and the scorn so that we could be <u>in</u> the Rose of Sharon.

He is God in all circumstances. Our peace is dependent on Him, not on the thorns around us, but the beauty of the Rose of Sharon.

Read Romans 5: 1

We have peace with God because we are justified through faith in Jesus. What does that mean? For years we have stressed the simplicity of salvation but have ignored the complexity involved. It's a paradox. Salvation is indeed given freely to all who by simple faith accept Jesus Christ as the propitiation for their sin. We are not saved by human effort yet we must be willing to yield our lives to Him. We are freely given salvation but we must freely give our lives to Him. I stayed with my grandchildren for several days while their parents were out of town. I don't really know why, but one of them was having a really difficult time. She was angry with anyone who crossed her path and especially with me. (Admittedly, I could have handled it better. Still praying about how I should have responded.) Her siblings tried to tell her to apologize to me, but that just made her angrier with them. She absolutely refused to get up to go to school, so the others left for school while she was locked in her room (her choice, not mine). As I picked up clothes and toys in the foyer, I noticed a beautifully colored paper airplane among the mess. Inside was a note that said, "I am sorry." I went upstairs and hugged her. I don't know if she was sincere or not. In retrospect I suspect that the apology was more to get out of trouble than it was an act of true repentance, because her attitude did not change for very long. We do the same thing spiritually sometimes. We recognize that we are sinful and need God's forgiveness, but are not truly repentant enough to be willing to allow Him to completely change us. While as a Nanna, I wanted the relationship with my granddaughter to be restored, I could not know her heart, only her actions. God is far superior to us. Not only does

He want our relationship with Him to be restored, He made the sacrifice in order for us to have the opportunity to come to Him in repentance. He also knows our hearts. Salvation is not coming forward and shaking the pastor's hand because someone we care about wants us to. It is not about being sorry we were caught in our sinfulness. It is not about avoiding punishment. Although that is a result, it is not the primary component. We are saved when we acknowledge our sinful state, repent and commit to yield our lives to Him in humble obedience. Salvation is a gift that changes us completely, not by our own effort but by a true yielding to God to work in us. We have peace with God when we are justified by sincere and life changing faith in Jesus Christ, our Savior, our Lord, and the Propitiation for our sin.

CHAPTER 9

JESUS MAKES US DIFFERENT

A wholehearted commitment to Christ means we are different than we were before we accepted Him as Savior and acknowledged Him.

Read Colossians 1:21-22. What does this scripture say about Christ's purpose in reconciling us?

Colossians 1:21-22 New International Version (NIV) 21 Once you were alienated from God and were enemies in your minds because of your evil behavior. 22 But now he has reconciled you by Christ's physical body through death to present you holy in his sight, without blemish and free from accusation—

Christ reconciled us so that He can present us holy to Himself. He covered all our ugliness and freed us from accusations. Without Him we were justly accused. With Him, we are no longer subjected to accusations.

HOLY, WITHOUT BLEMISH, BLAMELESS

Read Ephesians 5:25-27

This scripture is often used as the basis for lessons on the marriage relationship and is an excellent basis for any marriage. However, let's focus on what this passage says about God's love for us, His church. He gave Himself up for us, so that He could make us holy. We often say that He died so that we could be saved. That only scratches the surface. He died and resurrected so that He could wash us through the word, present us to Himself radiant, without stain, without wrinkles, without blemish, holy, and blameless.

Do some self-examination? Are you radiant, without stain, without wrinkles, without blemish, holy, and blameless?

In our sinful nature, none of us are holy, blameless or without blemish. We have been having some plumbing issues that affect our hot water. Yesterday, I really needed to take a shower and wash my hair, but it was 20 degrees outside, 60 degrees in my bathroom, and we didn't have any hot water. I heated enough water on the stove to wet a washcloth, and put my hair in a ponytail, but did not go to school looking or smelling all that great. When we examine our physical condition, we are not perfect by any stretch of the imagination. How much worse is our spiritual condition without Christ. Yet because of His love for us, He presents us to Himself miraculously clean, perfect, and holy.

There are a few things that we must DO, not to gain or secure our salvation but as obedient acts of faith in Him.

Colossians 1:23 New International Version (NIV) 23 if you continue in your faith, established and firm, and do not move from the hope held out in the gospel. This is the gospel that you heard and that has been proclaimed to every creature under heaven, and of which I, Paul, have become a servant.

What does God want us to do because of what He has done for us?

REMAIN GROUNDED

Read 1 Corinthians 1:5-9

It seems that everywhere we have lived, there have been issues with houses not having a firm foundation. One town had a type of soil that would cause damage to the foundation of your house if it became too dry. (D. Smith) People actually watered their houses. I still think that sounds so strange, but necessary because it could cost thousands of dollars to have your house "leveled" or the cracks in the foundation repaired. Another town was built near a fault line that would shift slightly. One day a door wouldn't stay closed. The next it closed perfectly. The next day it wouldn't close at all. Another town was built over old coal mines. Mine subsidence (Illinois Mine Subsidence Insurance Fund) could cause your house to fall into the ground. A house in a neighborhood near ours sank several inches into the ground overnight. I am sure the residents of that house would tell you the importance of having a firm foundation. Let's consider, not only the physical earth under our feet or our houses, but the very foundation of our walk with Christ.

How does Jesus keep us firm until the end?

I know that by now you are familiar with the phrase "in Him" so let's look at what these verses tell us about how being IN Him keeps us firm. Because of His grace, we have fellowship with Him. Through this fellowship with Him, He enriches us in every way. Somewhere in my education, someone warned me about using words like "never" and "always" because there are exceptions and extenuating circumstances that could affect the accuracy of these words. No teacher ever warned me about using the word "every". However, in human terms, "every" is also a dangerous word. Not with God. What He says is <u>always</u> true. He <u>never</u> lies. When He tells us that Jesus enriches us in <u>every way</u>, we can accept that as absolute truth. He enriches our speech.

I am a true introvert. Old timers would have called me "backward" in my childhood. I was extremely shy. I can remember as a high school senior being intimidated by the 7th graders in the hallway. Really. I never made eye contact with others in the hallways. Being outgoing is still out of my comfort zone, but Jesus has enriched my speech and enabled me to speak publicly, in women's Bible studies, local in-service training in my job, and even multiple times to a gymnasium full of women at weekend events. He also enriches our knowledge. My husband did not put any effort into his high school education. He just didn't care. When he walked across the stage at high school graduation, his folder that should have held the diploma was empty. But God had other plans. Not only does he have his diploma, he also has a bachelor's degree, Master of Divinity, and a Doctorate in Ministry. He is a knowledgeable teacher and pastor. God has definitely enriched his knowledge. Jesus gives us every spiritual gift we need to stand firm in our commitment to Him.

Why does Jesus keep us firm until the end?

Our firm commitment to Him and the ways that He enriches us in every way serve as confirmation of our testimony about Him to others around us. When the Lord returns, or when we die, He presents us blameless before God because of His work in our lives.

Read 1 Corinthians 15:58

1 Corinthians 15: 58 shows us several components in standing firm. It never ceases to amaze me that even the things we need to do to grow spiritually are only possible by a dependence on God. Doing is not doing at all. Doing is yielding to Him. Doing is resting in Him. Doing is giving to Him. Doing is knowing Him. We stand firm by letting absolutely nothing move us away from Jesus. We should not let anything distract us and take our attention and commitment away from Him. Since I am a wife and mother/grandmother, work full time, am a part time postgraduate student, and involved in church activities, I need to remain focused on Him because there are so many things that can distract me. If you list the hats you wear, you also have multiple distractions.

Sometimes the distractions aren't even the big things. Right now we are under a winter weather advisory. I love snow. I want to focus on what God is saying to me in this study, but I am distracted by updated weather forecasts.

What distractions move you away from Jesus? Ask God to keep your focus on Him.

Look at the last part of 1 Corinthians 15:58. See the word "always." No exceptions. Not just sometimes. Always give yourself fully to the work of God. Every moment of every day we should be allowing God to work in us. Look back at the things we listed as distractions. We can either let them distract us or we can let God work in us in them. Give yourself fully. There is no holding back in giving ourselves fully. We are "all in." Just as He gave Himself for us, we give ourselves fully for His work. Let's look briefly at the propositions again. The work of God. Not our work for God. We should not be attempting to do things for Him. We should be yielding so that He can do His work in us and through us. Then, and only then, can we have confidence that our labor is not in vain.

Do you ever feel like your labor is in vain?

I admit it. When I do the laundry, clean the kitchen, pull weeds out of the flowerbed, or vacuum the floor, I feel like my labor is in vain. But my focus should not be on the perpetual piles of dirty laundry, dirty dishes, or weeds. My focus should be on allowing God to use me in these seemingly never ending "menial" tasks. Nothing we do is menial when God is working through us. When we give ourselves fully to His work, our labor is not in vain.

REMAIN STEADFAST IN THE FAITH

PRAY FOR FAITH

Read Luke 17:5

Even our faith is dependent on a willingness to yield to God. He is the One who increases our faith. We just have to ask Him to do so. Notice that I did not say "All we have to do is ask." When we ask, we need to be willing and prepared for however He works in us to increase our faith. When we look back through the scriptures at the lives of those people we consider giants of the faith, we see that they faced tests of their faith, trials, disappointments, and hardships. Their faith grew as they trusted God, not only in the times He blessed them with "good" times, but also in those circumstances that were difficult and discouraging. We jokingly say, "Don't pray for patience because 'the trying of your faith worketh patience'". (James 1:3) But it really should not be a joke. A wholehearted commitment to Him means that we are completely yielded to Him, want our faith to increase, and willingly allow God to work in our lives to bring that about.

Are you willing to pray for God to increase your faith? Take a moment to yield yourself to Him, asking Him to increase your faith. If you aren't ready to do that, pray that He will tender your heart to be yielded to Him.

HEAR SOUND TEACHING

Read Romans 10:17

Faith comes from hearing the message through the word of Christ. It is of utmost importance for us to hear God's Word taught. It is incumbent on us to search out sound teaching and apply it to our lives. Through the years I have heard people comment about what they consider important about their church experience. I haven't kept statistics, but it seems that music and fellowship are more frequent responses than sound doctrine. I do not know the origin of this quote, but I have heard it said, "It is easier to change the doctrine of a church than to change the music." The Bible teaches us that fellowship with other believers is important. Fellowship that encourages us in our relationship with God is vital. Scripture also provides numerous examples of worship through music. Songs with lyrics which are scripturally sound bring joy to God as we worship Him. I am not saying that these are not important to our spiritual growth, but our fellowship and our music must be scripturally sound or they are a deterrent rather than a support for spiritual growth. For our faith to grow, we need to hear <u>Biblical</u> teaching, have <u>Biblical</u> fellowship, and worship with <u>Biblical</u> songs and hymns.

James 3: 1 reminds us that those who presume to teach will be judged more strictly. I take that seriously, and my heartfelt prayer is that the words I have written in this study are sound doctrine and scripturally accurate. I also pray that God will use these words to bring you closer to Him as He increases your faith. That being said, the concept of sound Biblical teaching is a soapbox issue for me. So much of our teaching in churches is shallow at best and unscriptural at worst. Those of you who are teachers have an enormous responsibility and will be held accountable for what you teach. All of us, those who are teachers and those who are not, need to be keenly aware of the teaching we hear. Make sure that you are hearing and teaching sound doctrine.

THROUGH CHRIST'S POWER

Read 1 Corinthians 2:4-6

Remaining steadfast in our faith is not dependent on intelligence or education. We remain steadfast through Christ's power and His wisdom. Many professors in our institutions of higher learning openly ridicule those who place their faith in God. I have heard, but do not know the origins of the quote, that even among those who serve full time in some church related capacity, the higher their level of education, the less likely they are to believe that the Bible is God's inerrant, infallible Word. If true, that is indeed a sad statistic. I have known people with developmental disabilities who have steadfast faith in God. I have also known highly educated people whose faith is steadfast, not because of their education but because of God's power. Knowledge does not keep us steadfast. God does. We remain steadfast through Christ's power which leads to a mature wisdom, not based on intellect, education, or secular knowledge, but wholly on God's power and wisdom. Listen to the point here. When we are dependent on God's power to have steadfast faith, He grows us to maturity. The result of His power will also be His wisdom.

DISCIPLINE

Read Colossians 2:5-7

Parents discipline their children in the hope that the children will learn correct behavior and attitudes. The goal is for children to develop self-discipline and control their own actions. Paul is delighted in how disciplined the believers at Colossae are. The discipline in which Paul delighted was neither outward discipline nor self-discipline. The disciplined lives they lived were based on their firm faith and the results of Christ in their lives. As we look at these verses in Colossians 2: 5-7, notice the pattern. "Continue to live your lives…" There is a continuous progression of growth. The believers at Colossae had accepted Christ, were rooted in Him, built up in Him, strengthened their faith, overflowing with thanksgiving, lived lives of discipline which helped them to continue in Him, which rooted them in Him …The discipline we have as believers is not a discipline that comes from our own power. Our actions reflect Christ (are disciplined) as we continue to yield to His work in our lives.

FOCUS ON CHRIST

Read Hebrews 12:2

As a parent, a homeschool mom, grandparent, Sunday School teacher, and as a speech language pathologist, more times than I can count, I have said these words and phrases. "Look at me." "Focus." "Listen." "Let me see your eyes" is my go-to phrase. It seems to be more effective. I wanted them to pay attention because I had something that would help them. Looking at this scripture, I wonder if Jesus has often said these same phrases to me. I may have had valuable information or activities to increase the children's abilities in some skill areas, but Jesus is the perfecter of our faith. I may have life experience or education to qualify me to help the children, but Jesus is God who sacrificed Himself on the cross and sits at the right hand of the throne of God. If we are to remain steadfast in our faith, we must focus our eyes on the perfecter of our faith. Listen to Jesus ask you, "Let me see your eyes." Fix your eyes on Him.

FOLLOW GODLY EXAMPLES

Read Hebrews 13:7

I remember the names of my pastors and teachers when I was a child. I remember their lives. Sadly, I don't remember specific things about their teaching. The person I remember most as having influenced my life for Christ is my daddy. He spoke the word of God to me. Every day in our home and in his workplace, I saw his consistent faith and commitment to studying God's word. He was not perfect but I saw the outcome of his life and I hope to imitate his faith. As an adult I have encountered many leaders (teachers, deacons, church staff, friends) whose way of life has influenced me. Notice that the writer of Hebrews does not say for us to imitate their every action. Our leaders are human and make mistakes. We are to notice the outcome of their faith and imitate their way of life. Truthfully, this is somewhat frightening for me as a teacher and a pastor's wife. The thought that someone might be imitating me is overwhelming. If you are in a place where people look to you for leadership, you likely feel the same way. If you are looking to others as your leaders, remember that they will fail you from time to time. Look at the overall outcomes of their lives as they submit to God and imitate their way of life, not their specific actions.

NOT BE SHIFTED AWAY FROM THE HOPE

SCRIPTURE

Read Romans 15:4

Look at Romans 15: 4 again. How do we have hope?

In the context of scripture, hope is better translated as assurance. We have the assurance of Jesus' promises through the scriptures and the encouragement we receive through reading and studying the scriptures. Many years ago, at a Women's Conference in Memphis, a speaker whose name I only remember as "Johnetta" introduced me to a habit I have practiced periodically for years. She suggested reading five Psalms a day based on the day of the month plus 30, plus 30, plus 30, etc. For example, today is the 21ˢᵗ, so I would read Psalms 21, 51, 81, 111, and 141. This practice has encouraged me through many trials. The psalmists experienced all the trials, fears, and emotions I experience. They also recognized the Who of who God Is and worshiped in complete dependence. As I have mentioned previously, the books of prophecy were a great encouragement to me when we didn't know where our daughter was. One of God's purposes in revealing Himself to us in scripture is to give us a hope (assurance) that endures.

Think of times when the scriptures have encouraged you and given you hope (assurance) of God's promises.

HOLY SPIRIT

Read Romans 15:13

God is the God of Hope. Paul tells the believers at Colossae not to be shifted away from their hope. When we remember that God is our hope, we can understand this scripture to mean that we are not to be shifted away from God Himself. When God the Holy Spirit fills our lives, His power fills us to overflowing with His Hope. To be overflowing with hope, we are filled to capacity with God's Spirit. We must yield ourselves to God's Spirit and the resulting overflow will be hope (assurance.) My parents had a pond dug on our farm when I was a child. There are three natural springs on the floor of the pond. The pond quickly filled with bubbling clean water. Even in periods of drought, the pond was filled with water. Over the years sediment and cow manure among other things have sunk to the bottom of the pond. The pond is about 6 feet shallower now than it was originally. The water is often muddy. When there is little rain, the water level in the pond goes down. Why is that? Dirt has covered up the springs so that even though the springs are still there, the water does not freely flow to fill the pond. For His hope to overflow in us, we must not allow sin to fill us with dirt that keeps the hope from filling us completely.

SCRIPTURAL TEACHING

Read 2 Thessalonians 2:15-17

God is the source of our hope. His motivation for providing us with this assurance is His grace and His love. He uses others to teach us as He works in us. Paul tells the church in Thessalonica to stand firm and to hold on to what they had been taught. The result of remembering and applying sound scriptural teaching is that God encourages us and gives us assurance (hope.) He also strengthens us so that our actions and our words reflect Him. Our words and actions teach others, encourage others, strengthen others. Isn't it amazing how the circle continues. Last week I was trying to remember the name of a song we sang in Sunday School when I was in elementary school. I sent a social media message to friends from that era and asked if they remembered the song. That began a discussion about all the teachers at church who had influenced our lives by their teaching and their example. We may not remember everything they taught us, but their legacy lives on. I pray that God will use me to influence others' words and actions, that others will remember how God used my teaching, and that He will use me to encourage hearts and remind them of the Hope they have in Him.

Take a moment to remember the teaching you have heard. Are you encouraged and strengthened in the assurance you have in Christ?

GOD OUR SAVIOR

Read 1 Timothy 4:10

The basis of our hope and the provider of our hope is our Savior, God incarnate Jesus Christ. Everything we do is because of the hope we have in God. How simple yet so life changing. Think about the preceding statements in practical terms. God gives us hope not only of forgiveness of our sin, of relationship and fellowship with Him, but also in our everyday tasks. He is our hope in our jobs, our chores, our recreation, our ministries, our friendships. He is our Hope in everything we do and say. When I have a student climbing on chairs, rearranging the furniture and talking constantly because he didn't take his medicine, God is my hope. When my husband is in another wreck, God is my hope. When I think I have made a big mistake at work, God is my hope. When I have graduate school assignments due and I feel overwhelmed, God is my hope. (Yes, every one of those things happened **this** week, and God is my unwavering Hope.) Our hope is steadfast and unwavering only when we remember Who is our Hope.

Pause and remember that God is your unfailing Hope in everything you experience. Thank Him.

GOD'S PROMISES

Read Hebrews 10:22-23

Our hope is unwavering and steadfast because we <u>know</u> by faith that God is faithful to keep all His promises. I have seen a book that claims to list 5000 promises of God. I don't know exactly how many promises God gives us. Five thousand may be a conservative estimate. Let's look at the ones listed in Hebrews 10: 22. Because of His promise and His gift, we can approach Him. Our sin is forgiven by His sacrificial death, His blood, and we can draw near to Him with confidence. Have you ever felt like anyone in your life was unapproachable? Someone who made you feel like spending time with you was an inconvenience? Someone who would tell you what you wanted to hear just to get rid of you with no intention of following through? Those things never happen with God. We draw near to Him with assurance that He wants us to come to Him in faith with a sincere heart and that He will follow through with every promise He has given us.

CHAPTER 10

PAUL'S EXAMPLE

How does this type of total, wholehearted commitment occur? Ultimately through Christ. But we also recognize the sacrifice other humans have made so that we could hear the gospel. These people had wholehearted devotion to our Savior. Their lives were not always easy. In fact, many suffered persecution, torture and martyrdom for His kingdom. But they knew everything they suffered was worth it because they knew who Christ is. And the blessing in this is that we can continue their legacy when our wholehearted devotion brings others to Him, and they, in turn, are devoted to Him and bring others to Him. We often use the term "vicious cycle" to denote a pattern of sin and despair. Oh, the joy of the thought that we can begin a "blessed cycle" that can change those patterns of sin. Paul, the writer of Colossians serves as an example for us.

In Paul's statements in Colossians 1: 24-29 we see some of Paul's characteristics.

Colossians 1:24-29 New International Version (NIV) 24 Now I rejoice in what I am suffering for you, and I fill up in my flesh what is still lacking in regard to Christ's afflictions, for the sake of his body, which is the church. 25 I have become its servant by the commission God gave me to present to you the word of God in its fullness— 26 the mystery that has been kept hidden for ages and generations, but is now disclosed to the Lord's people. 27 To them God has chosen to make known among the Gentiles the glorious riches of this mystery, which is Christ in you, the hope of glory. 28 He is the one we proclaim, admonishing and teaching everyone with all wisdom, so that we may present everyone fully mature in Christ. 29 To this end I strenuously contend with all the energy Christ so powerfully works in me.

List some of the characteristics Paul lists about himself in these verses.

- Rejoicing in suffering and afflictions
- Making God's message fully known
  - the glorious wealth of this mystery
  - Christ in you, the hope of glory
- Proclaiming Him

- Warning and teaching everyone with wisdom
- Present everyone mature
- Labor with His strength that works powerfully in us

I sometimes think I would have liked to know Paul personally, but I am sure I would have been intimidated by him. And he would likely have reprimanded me for my failures to serve wholeheartedly. He penned much of the New Testament and started churches throughout Asia Minor. From scripture we know much about how Paul viewed himself, and many of the things he did and places he went. He had a death-to-self humility yet tremendous confidence in the work of Christ in him. In this passage in Colossians 1: 24-29, as with all scripture it is imperative that we do not take any one passage out of context. Here Paul is expressing his confidence in the purpose God had for him. Do not be tempted to think that he was egotistical. Before Christ revealed Himself to him, Paul/Saul persecuted believers. He never forgot what he had done and how merciful God had been to him in showing him the Truth. The list of adjectives I would use to describe Paul is long and sometimes seems contradictory.

Look at each of the following scriptures. What adjective would you use to describe Paul based on each passage?

Read Acts 7:57-8:1

Based on Acts 7: 57-8:1, how would you describe Saul/Paul?

I do not know the significance of the witnesses laying their coats at the feet of Saul. Perhaps it means nothing. Perhaps it has great significance. But scripture is clear that the young Saul approved of the stoning of Stephen. Simply put, he approved of the murder of an innocent man. At this point he was not actively involved in the killing, but we will see that this was the beginning of an escalation in his persecution of believers. Schools do not tolerate bullying. As a public-school employee, I was required to watch a series of videos on preventing bullying. One of the issues addressed concerned teaching other children not to stand idly by when they see another child being bullied. Children are encouraged to stand up for the victims of bullying. Bullying does not even begin to compare to what was happening to Stephen, yet not only did Saul stand idly by and watch it happen, he approved of it. From this passage I would describe him standing on the edge of evil, yet believing his evil to be good. We know from other scripture that he was educated by the prestigious religious law instructor Gamaliel. (Acts 22: 3) We know that he was zealous for the law but did not understand God's grace. (I want to make a distinction here before we continue. There is a difference between the Levitical law that God gave to Moses, and the Pharisaic law. The Pharisees had written detailed ways to keep the Levitical law. I liken this to the difference between the laws that our Congress makes and the regulations written by the bureaucracies that implement and enforce the laws. Paul had a zeal for the Pharisaic law.)

Read Acts 9:1-2

Based on Acts 9: 1-2, how would you describe Paul?

Paul was obsessed with destroying everyone who believed in Christ and had accepted the gift of salvation available through His sacrificial death and resurrection. He was breathing out murderous threats. I can imagine the fire in his eyes and his aggressive posture. He was filled with hate. He was scary. His zeal for the Pharisaic law had consumed and corrupted him so that his religion had made him evil.

Read Acts 9:17-22

Based on Acts 9: 17-22, how would you describe Paul?

He had been breathing out murderous threats about the believers. Now he is powerfully proving that Jesus is the Messiah. How would I describe him in these verses? Changed. Miraculously changed. He had zealously persecuted believers in Christ. Now he wholeheartedly follows Christ.

*Please take the time to read **Acts 13- Acts 28** in your Bible or on your Bible app. How would you describe Paul based on these chapters? Think about how God used this changed man to change the world. Consider how God has used you in the world around you. Pray for God to work through you to make a difference.*

The Pauline Epistles (letters written by Paul) also give insight into Paul's life.

Read Philippians 3:4-10

Based on Philippians 3: 4-10, how would you describe Paul?

Paul was aware of how his education, his genealogical heritage, and his religious zeal would be viewed in the Jewish religious community. He would have been pretty important. When he surrendered his life to Christ, he gave up a successful religious career as a Pharisee. He understood that the things he gave up were of absolutely no value. None. Those things were worthless. Those early accolades were garbage. Yesterday I walked out to the road to bring the garbage cans back to the house. I did not realize it because our son had taken the cans to the road, but some kind of varmint had gotten into the garbage and destroyed the trash bags. Garbage was loose in the cans. Since our trash service only takes bagged garbage, they did not pick up our trash. Then, it had rained. It was *nasty*. Now, think about this nasty garbage. This is how Paul viewed the things he gave up to follow Christ. He understood that any perceived righteousness based on the culture of his day, because of family heritage, religious upbringing, prestigious education, and self-discipline of following the Pharisaic law was worthless when compared to the righteousness he received through Christ. He wanted to be like Christ. He wanted His power, even though he knew that involved sharing in His suffering and dying to self.

Read 1 Timothy 1:15-16

Based on 1 Timothy 1: 15-16, how would you describe Paul?

Remember that we began this section with another scripture in which Paul gave a detailed description of himself. The descriptions in Colossians 1: 24-29 and 1 Timothy 1: 15-16 may sound quite different at first reading, but both scriptures give a clear description of how Paul viewed himself. These descriptions are not contradictory at all. In writing to Timothy Paul explains how he could do and be the things described in Colossians 1. He humbly recognizes his own sinfulness. As he remembered his former life, I can imagine the guilt he must have felt at times, and how thankful he was for the mercy and grace shown to him through Jesus. He also recognized that because of the miraculous change in his life, Jesus could use him as an example to others. Paul wasn't on display. Jesus was on display in Paul. As a homeschool family we have made field trips to some really interesting places. When we go to a museum, we often look into a display case at some archeological find or an item preserved for its historical significance. The case is not on display. The item is on display. Jesus was on display in Paul. When people looked at Paul, they saw Jesus' mercy, grace, patience and power. Because Paul recognized his own sinfulness, died to self and allowed Jesus to put Himself on display through him, Paul could confidently say the things he said in Colossians 1: 24-29.

*Please use your Bible or your Bible app to read **2 Corinthians 11**. Paul is using a human argument to make his point. What do you learn from this chapter?*

Paul was humbly realistic. He realized how the Jewish community viewed his earthly qualifications. He admitted his own sinfulness. He acknowledged the persecution and suffering he had endured because of his obedience to Christ. He spoke of the self-sacrifices he had made for others. He recognized the work that Jesus did through him. To deny that would be to deny the power of God. He boasted <u>only</u> in what Christ had done in and through him. We too need to be realistic. On

Fridays my schedule allows me to work on paperwork and planning. Sometimes I am overwhelmed and don't have nearly enough time to do what needs to be done. This particular Friday I seemed to be caught up on everything that I could. However, I couldn't do some other things that needed to be done because I was waiting on a colleague to do some things first. In asking myself why there wasn't anything for me to do, I told myself, "I'm just that good." Then I laughed. That was not realistic thinking. There are times when I am <u>really</u> not good at all, but there are times when I can be fairly efficient. You are that way too. I know this because it is the case for all humans. We acknowledge that in earthly things. We are realistic. We must do the same spiritually. We recognize our state of sinfulness and inadequacy but we cannot deny the work of God in us. If we deny what He does in us, we show our ingratitude and diminish His display of His power, mercy, grace and patience in us. Paul could boast only in Christ. We should do the same.

Read Romans 7:14-25

How would you describe Paul based on Romans 7: 14-25?

Paul struggled. His testimony of the struggles he faced to follow God wholeheartedly serves to encourage us. When I read his words, I feel that they are my own words. You probably do too. The word I would use to describe Paul from these verses is "human." In the book of Acts, we read about the miraculous change God worked in him, the results of all the work God did through him, and his powerful teaching. We read about his endurance in suffering. In the Pauline epistles we read his words of rebuke, encouragement, and instruction. It is easy to forget he shared the same struggles we have. He wanted to be more yielded to God's work in his life. He was tempted and yielded to temptation. Yet he delighted in God's law, the law of grace and liberty. God used him. Because of his humanness, God used him. God delivered him through Jesus Christ. God can deliver and use sinful me when I yield to Him. God can deliver and use sinful you when you yield to Him. Be encouraged that God will deliver us too.

We have only touched on some of Paul's life and his testimony. As you read the history of the early church as chronicled in the book of Acts, you see how he lived his life. As you read the letters he wrote to the churches, you see more of how he described himself and how he encouraged other believers.

As I write these last words in the study, I feel a sadness to be leaving our conversation, a blessing that God has allowed me this time with you, and a relief that this particular task has been completed. I do not know if God will lead me to write again, but if He does not, I have enjoyed this time. I am leaving you with some scripture references and some questions to ask/answer on your own. I hope that you will continue to study. The questions that follow are intended to help you relate to

Paul and to other people who God used in scripture to carry out His work on planet earth. Listen to God and yield wholeheartedly to the lessons He teaches you through scripture.

1. *What words does scripture use to tell us the condition of Paul's heart?*
2. *Who or what influenced Paul positively in his relationship with God? What lessons can we learn?*
3. *Who or what influenced Paul negatively in his relationship with God? What lessons can we learn?*
4. *What disciplines or hardships did Paul experience? Why?*
5. *What blessings did God give Paul because of his commitment to Him?*
6. *How did sin affect his relationship with God?*
7. *Consider his entire life. What lessons can we learn and how can we apply those to our lives?*

FOR FURTHER STUDY

In this final section we will do some character studies. For each person listed, we have some basic scriptures to read and some questions to answer. Up to this point we have studied what it means to be wholeheartedly committed to Christ. By examining the lives of real people who, to some extent were committed to God, yet were fallible and made some significant mistakes, we can draw some conclusions and make some applications as to how we can live wholeheartedly and avoid some of the pitfalls they experienced.

CALEB
Numbers 13:30-14:38
Joshua 14:6-15:19
Judges 1: 12-20

1. *What words does scripture use to tell us the condition of Caleb's heart?*
2. *Who or what influenced Caleb positively in his relationship with God? What lessons can we learn?*
3. *Who or what influenced Caleb negatively in his relationship with God? What lessons can we learn?*
4. *How did sin affect his relationship with God?*
5. *What disciplines or hardships did Caleb experience? Why?*
6. *What blessings did God give Caleb because of his commitment to Him?*
7. *Consider his entire life. What lessons can we learn and how can we apply those to our lives?*

DAVID
1 Samuel 16:1–1 Kings 2: 11
1 Chronicles 11: 1–1 Chronicles 29:29

1 Kings 15:5 New International Version (NIV) 5 For David had done what was right in the eyes of the Lord and had not failed to keep any of the Lord's commands all the days of his life—except in the case of Uriah the Hittite.

Acts 13:22 King James Version (KJV) 22 And when he had removed him, he raised up unto them David to be their king; to whom also he gave their testimony, and said, I have found David the son of Jesse, a man after mine own heart, which shall fulfil all my will.

1. *What words does scripture use to tell us the condition of David's heart?*
2. *Who or what influenced David positively in his relationship with God? What lessons can we learn?*
3. *Who or what influenced David negatively in his relationship with God? What lessons can we learn?*
4. *How did sin affect his relationship with God?*
5. *What disciplines or hardships did he experience? Why?*
6. *What blessings did God give him because of his commitment to Him?*
7. *Consider his entire life. What lessons can we learn and how can we apply those to our lives?*

The next character studies will be about some of the kings who followed King David. The scripture references will be shorter and we will not have as much information available to draw our conclusions.

ASA
1 Kings 15:9-24
2 Chronicles 14-16

1. *What words does scripture use to tell us the condition of Asa's heart?*
2. *Who or what influenced Asa positively in his relationship with God? What lessons can we learn?*
3. *Who or what influenced Asa negatively in his relationship with God? What lessons can we learn?*
4. *How did sin affect his relationship with God?*
5. *What disciplines or hardships did Asa experience? Why?*
6. *What blessings did God give Asa because of his commitment to Him?*
7. *Consider his entire life. What lessons can we learn and how can we apply those to our lives?*

JEHOSHAPHAT

- **1 Kings 15: 24**
- **I Kings 22**
- **2 Kings 3**
- **2 Chronicles 17-20**

1. *What words does scripture use to tell us the condition of Jehoshaphat's heart?*
2. *Who or what influenced Jehoshaphat positively in his relationship with God? What lessons can we learn?*

3. *Who or what influenced Jehoshaphat negatively in his relationship with God? What lessons can we learn?*
4. *How did sin affect his relationship with God?*
5. *What disciplines or hardships did he experience? Why?*
6. *What blessings did God give him because of his commitment to Him?*
7. *Consider his entire life. What lessons can we learn and how can we apply those to our lives?*

JOASH

Joash was not an exceptional example, but look at his life and the mistakes he made. He followed God only as long as his mentor was alive.

- **2 Kings 11-12,**
- **2 Chronicles 22, 24- 25**

1. *What words does scripture use to tell us the condition of Joash's heart?*
2. *Who or what influenced Joash positively in his relationship with God? What lessons can we learn?*
3. *Who or what influenced Joash negatively in his relationship with God? What lessons can we learn?*
4. *How did sin affect his relationship with God?*
5. *What disciplines or hardships did he experience? Why?*
6. *What blessings did God give him because of his commitment to Him?*
7. *Consider his entire life. What lessons can we learn and how can we apply those to our lives?*

AMAZIAH

- **2 Kings 14**
- **2 Chronicles 25**

1. *What words does scripture use to tell us the condition of Amaziah's heart?*
2. *Who or what influenced Amaziah positively in his relationship with God? What lessons can we learn?*
3. *Who or what influenced Amaziah negatively in his relationship with God? What lessons can we learn?*
4. *How did sin affect his relationship with God?*
5. *What disciplines or hardships did he experience? Why?*
6. *What blessings did God give him because of his commitment to Him?*
7. *Consider his entire life. What lessons can we learn and how can we apply those to our lives?*

AZARIAH

- **2 Kings 15: 1-7**

1. *What words does scripture use to tell us the condition of Azariah's heart?*
2. *Who or what influenced Azariah positively in his relationship with God? What lessons can we learn?*
3. *Who or what influenced Azariah negatively in his relationship with God? What lessons can we learn?*
4. *How did sin affect his relationship with God?*
5. *What disciplines or hardships did he experience? Why?*
6. *What blessings did God give him because of his commitment to Him?*
7. *Consider his entire life. What lessons can we learn and how can we apply those to our lives?*

JOTHAM

- **2 Kings 15: 32-38**
- **2 Chronicles 27: 1-9**

1. *What words does scripture use to tell us the condition of Jotham's heart?*
2. *Who or what influenced Jotham positively in his relationship with God? What lessons can we learn?*
3. *Who or what influenced Jotham negatively in his relationship with God? What lessons can we learn?*
4. *How did sin affect his relationship with God?*
5. *What disciplines or hardships did he experience? Why?*
6. *What blessings did God give him because of his commitment to Him?*
7. *Consider his entire life. What lessons can we learn and how can we apply those to our lives?*

HEZEKIAH

- **2 Kings 18-20**
- **2 Chronicles 29-32**
- **Isaiah 36-39**
- **Jeremiah 26: 18-19**

1. *What words does scripture use to tell us the condition of Hezekiah's heart?*
2. *Who or what influenced Hezekiah positively in his relationship with God? What lessons can we learn?*

3. *Who or what influenced Hezekiah negatively in his relationship with God? What lessons can we learn?*
4. *How did sin affect his relationship with God?*
5. *What disciplines or hardships did he experience? Why?*
6. *What blessings did God give him because of his commitment to Him?*
7. *Consider his entire life. What lessons can we learn and how can we apply those to our lives?*

JOSIAH
1 Kings 13: 1-3
2 Kings 21:24 – 2 Kings 23: 34
2 Chronicles 33: 25 – 2 Chronicles 35: 26

1. *What words does scripture use to tell us the condition of Josiah's heart?*
2. *Who or what influenced Josiah positively in his relationship with God? What lessons can we learn?*
3. *Who or what influenced Josiah negatively in his relationship with God? What lessons can we learn?*
4. *How did sin affect his relationship with God?*
5. *What disciplines or hardships did he experience? Why?*
6. *What blessings did God give him because of his commitment to Him?*
7. *Consider his entire life. What lessons can we learn and how can we apply those to our lives?*

TIMOTHY
1 Timothy 4

1. *What words does scripture use to tell us the condition of Timothy's heart?*
2. *Who or what influenced Timothy positively in his relationship with God? What lessons can we learn?*
3. *Who or what influenced Timothy negatively in his relationship with God? What lessons can we learn?*
4. *What disciplines or hardships did he experience? Why?*
5. *What blessings did God give him because of his commitment to Him?*
6. *How did sin affect his relationship with God?*
7. *Consider his entire life. What lessons can we learn and how can we apply those to our lives?*

EPILOGUE

It's been nearly 6 years since I wrote this Bible study. Truthfully, things have been too busy for me to pursue getting it published, or more likely, it just wasn't in God's perfect timing.

Lots of things have changed. My husband's health continued to decline. He was forced to retire from his part time pastorate. He was devastated because he lived (and loved) to preach and teach God's Word. He had all confidence that God's purpose for him was to prepare God's people for works of service. When he was in hospice, I retired to be with him in his last days. Sadly, he died only 9 days after my retirement. Even though I miss him, I have complete peace that God's plan for him was completed. I currently attend the church where I grew up. I'm renewing old friendships and making new friends. After 40 plus years of having Bryan as my pastor, I'm thankful to have a pastor now who also preaches the Word with integrity and passion.

We have 2 more living grandchildren than we did at that time, and another grandchild who went to heaven before she was born. The little early morning person who shared a quiet time with me is a freshman in college. My daughter-in-law who was just diagnosed with carcinoid cancer when I wrote the study is doing well. She still has some health concerns, but overall is doing well. The son I mentioned who was military retired after 20 years of service. He has a successful second career that he enjoys. I miss the sweet children I saw when I worked as a speech language pathologist, but there is a time for everything, and that time has closed. Even though our children and grandchildren are scattered, I enjoy getting to see them and spend time with them.

ABOUT THE AUTHOR

Mary Lynne and her son live on the property homesteaded by her great-great grandfather. Her adult daughter lives across the road. She is active in her local church, where she is on the library committee and teaches Women's Bible studies.

Before her husband was forced to retire due to his health, Mary Lynne was a pastor's wife for over 40 years. She and her husband ministered in churches in Arkansas, Mississippi, Texas, and Illinois. Some of the ways she has ministered include leading Bible studies, cooking Wednesday night meals, presenting at women's retreats and children's camps, hosting staff and other various events in their home, teaching Sunday School classes.

They have been blessed with five adult children, and ten grandchildren: four grandchildren in Arkansas, three in Texas, two in North Carolina, and one in heaven. She is thankful for two wonderful daughters-in-law, and a wonderful son-in law. Spending time with her adult children, their spouses, and their children is one of her favorite things to do. Her grandchildren have varied interests: baseball, volleyball, ballet, choir, soccer, etc. Whatever they do, she enjoys watching them pursue their interests. She doesn't get to see them as often as she would like.

She has a bachelor's degree in Speech Therapy, a Master of Communicative Disorders in Speech Language Pathology, and an Educational Specialist Degree in Special Education Administration. In her professional career, she worked as a speech language pathologist in the public-school setting, early intervention services, and residential children's rehabilitation center. She has also worked as a therapy coordinator, assistant administrator in a residential rehab center, and as a special education coordinator. She has also home schooled her children.

Her hobbies include working in the yard, reading, and traveling to visit friends and family.

BIBLIOGRAPHY

Blackboard Jumble. By Daws Butler. Dir. Michael Lah. Perf. Voice over by Daws Butler, Joe Trescari Animated. 1957.

Brooks, Garth. "Standing Outside the Fire." *In Pieces.* By Jenny Yates Garth Brooks. Prod. Allen Reynolds. Nashville: Jack's Tracks, 1993.

Cash, Johnny. "No Earthly Good." *The Rambler.* By Johnny Cash. Prod. Jack Routh, Johnny Cash Charlie Bragg. Nashville: Columbia Records, 1977.

Chemistry of Emotions. n.d. <https://www.chemistryislife.com/the-chemistry-of-emotions>.

Davis, Mac. "It's Hard to Be Humble." *Casablanca.* cond. Larry Butler. By Mac Davis. 1980.

Eliza E. Hewitt, John R. Sweney. "Will There Be Any Stars in My Crown." *Baptist Sankey Hymnal.* 1897.

Fifth Sense. n.d. Birmingham Smell and Taste Group. 2018. <https://www.fifthsense.org.uk/psychology-and-smell/>.

Hee Haw. By John Aylesworth, Archie Campbell Frank Peppiatt. Nashville. 1969-1992.

Henry Blackaby, Richard Blackaby, Claude Smith. *Experiencing Bod.* Nashville, Tennessee: Baptist Sunday School Board (Lifeway), 1990.

Illinois Mine Subsidence Insurance Fund. n.d. <https://www.imsif.com/what-is-mine-subsidence/>.

Mars Attack. Dir. Tim Burton. Perf. Jack Nicholson. Prod. Larry J. Franco Tim Burton. 1996.

Ministries, David Ring. *David Ring.* n.d. <https://www.davidring.org/>.

Murphy, David lee. "Dust on the Bottle." *Out with a Bant.* By David Lee Murphy. Prod. Tony Brown. Nashville: MCA, 1995.

"New Oxford Dictionary." Merriam-Webster, 2018.

Sheldon, Garrett Ward, Charles Sheldon, Deborah Morris. *In His Steps*. B&H Publishing Group, 1897, 1935.

Smith, Cal. "The Lord Knows I'm Drinking." *I've Found Someone of My Won*. By Bill Anderson. Prod. Walter Haynes. Nashville: Decca, 1972.

Smith, Doug. *Clay soil results in a foundation of woes in Houston construction*. 28 August 2002. Houston Business Journal.

<https://www.bizjournals.com/houston/stories/2002/04/29/focus5.html>.

Smith, Michael. "Friends are Friends Forever." *The Michael W. Smith Project*. By Michael Smith Deborah Smith. BMG Rights Management, Capitol CMG Publishing, Warner Chappel Much, Inc., 1983.

The Bullwinkle Show, Rocky and Friends. By Jay Ward Bill Scott. Dir. Frank Braxton, Pete Burness Gerald Baldwin. Perf. Animated. Prod. Jay Ward and Bill Scholl. 1959-1964.

Toy Story. By Pete Docter, Andrew Stanton, Joe Ranft John Lasseter. Dir. William Reeves John Lasseter. Perf. voices by Tom Hanks, Till Allen, Don Rickles, Jim Varney, Wallace Shawn, Animated. Prod. Steve JobsKaren Robert Jackson Edwin Catmull. 1995.

Various. *Murphy's Law, Wilipedia*. n.d. Internet. 2018.

Wikipedia. *Language Center*. n.d. <https://en.wikipedia.org/wiki/Language_center>.